If My Vagina Could Talk...

By:

Lyndia Lipscomb

Co-Authors:

Destiny De La Rosa

Tricia Wolak

Rebecca Rockingham

Kimberley Grimes

Copyright © 2020 Lyndia Lipscomb

All rights reserved.

ISBN: 978-0-578-69539-6

Library of Congress Control Number: 2020938616

DEDICATION

This book is dedicated to the most powerful, strong, independent, and most beautiful women all over the Universe that have loved and cried all from the naturally given most powerful possession in the world; the Va-JJ.

FREEDOM OF SPEECH

The stories that you are about to read are written in each author's words. They are from places and times in their lives that were very painful, thoughtful, and/or joyous. Some verbiage may be explicit, but if it is what they felt and needed to say to explain their personal tragedy's and triumph's, then we allowed them to speak from the heart, the soul and of course the Va-JJ. We caution you not to judge but to embrace their journeys of life!

TABLE OF CONTENTS

Dedication iii

Freedom Of Speech iii

Acknowledgments 5

Introduction 6

Chapter 1: From $20 To $200 8

Chapter 2: The Quest Of A Gypsy 43

Chapter 3: Life On A Couch 59

Chapter 4: Me, Him, Them And Then I 82

Chapter 5: The Hair Slayer 89

About The Author 94

ACKNOWLEDGMENTS

There are so many beautiful women I have met that have been a great presence in my life and there has been so many strangers that have stepped up to assist me during my trials and tribulations. But most importantly I would like to thank my best friend for over 45 years Donna Rette and my daughter Nesa. These two keep me grounded and sane even when my anxiety kicks in, which is pretty much all the time. Also, I would profoundly like to thank and acknowledge my friends and the co-authors of this book: Rebecca, Tricia, Kimberley and Destiny. Without you ladies opening your hearts to reveal your own personal scars and healing of life this book may not have been possible. It took love and courage and for that you will always be beloved for your gift.

Special Thank You:

Nesa Kovacs – Cover Stylist
Jennifer Barrett – Photo Photographer
www.antheminart.com
Phyllis Brewer, Owner of TriVashion Boutique - Back Cover Hat
www.trivashion.com
Feign Boutique – Jewelry
www.feignboutique.com

INTRODUCTION

I am not one to knock religion or one's belief in the higher power, but I often wonder sometimes why the hell did Eve bite the apple. Was she hormonal or is it possible that she was born with this emotional creature that every woman carries inside: the vagina?

What is the vagina you ask? There are several meanings in the dictionary but here is the most popular meaning: The vagina is an elastic, muscular canal with a soft, flexible lining that provides lubrication and sensation. The vagina connects the uterus to the outside world. And that my friends are where it gets all twisted; connecting to the outside world which in my eyes, can turn in to this emotional, psychotic creature, that can change your life forever.

The word "vagina" comes from Latin and means "sheath for a sword." I guess that gives a whole new meaning to the saying: "Live by the sword, Die by the sword". Lawd if I knew that many years ago, I would have protected my vagina like the forbidden fruit. I mean I would have fed it avocado toast and cucumber sandwiches with the crust dipped in champagne.

But here is something you all should know; your vagina can fall out, like an inside-out sock. Do you want me to repeat that just in case you think you did not read it correctly? Yes, your vagina can fall out! The condition is called pelvic organ prolapse, and it's when your vagina begins to fall out of its normal position. It is caused by injury to the muscles or tissues that support the pelvic organs. The main cause of this injury is pregnancy and childbirth. If that is not the most emotional crisis to a woman, I don't know what is? I said all this to say that the vagina is tough, it's the presence of our being, it's the center of your soul, it can take a good pounding, and get fixed up to go thru life again.

Women are strong from the center soul of our being. Women are survivors, we are mothers, sisters, daughters, friends, grandmothers, wives, and more. But sometimes, our spirit, our center core, and our minds get clouded and even broken by the lives around us or the self-inflicted wounds we scar upon ourselves. But if you can revive yourself and rejuvenate your life to be this beautiful soul again and have the strength to find your purpose and the courage to love yourself and others again, than you have done what you were put on earth to do, and for that I commend your love for your own body, mind and soul.

And this my friends is what this book is about! It's about 5 courageous women that honorably peel back the layers of their skin to reveal their power, their strength and self-worth to rise above the bondage of their past.

I encourage every reader not to judge one's past or path, but to seek your own purpose in life to become an inspiring teacher to those that walk in your path of life.

Enjoy the Read!

Chapter 1

FROM $20 TO $200

~Lady LL.

Umm that was not as good as I thought it was going to be, but what the hell I just fucked a celebrity. As I lay here next to this tall dark and handsome BET famous comic, I sexually pushed my buttocks up in that warm cuddle spot in the cup of his body near that important spot. He starts to cup my buttocks and body. Yes, I am feeling this spooning position as he puts his arm over me to cuddle my body, then just as I feel comfortable, his arm reaches way over me and he reaches his hand into the pocket of his jeans that are lying next to me on the floor and he pulls out a twenty-dollar bill. I look at him and he kisses me softly on the neck as I hear a horn blow from outside his bottom floor apartment. He then says to me as he hands me the twenty-dollar bill: "Here, your cab is outside". What the fuck just happened? I was not sure but when the horn blew again, I just jumped up, with bra and underwear in tow, throwing my jeans on my body, and stepping back into my high heels, to run out the door. And no, he did not get up to see me to the door, he simply rolled over as I walked out the bedroom.

As I jumped in the cab, I thought to myself did this punk ass dude just give me twenty bucks for a fuck. Yep he sure did! All I could do was laugh at my self-worth. I had become a twenty-dollar hoe in my mid-twenties. I am a mom of two and a soon to be divorcee living single again, and I have literally managed to become a twenty-dollar hoe. What a great way to start my new single life after a fucked up and abusive marriage. How the hell did this happen?

All I remember is that when I was sixteen years old sitting on the floor with my cousins in North Carolina during our normal summer visits, watching Princess Diana and Prince Charles wed in Buckingham Palace, I imagined and believed that was going to happen to me. After watching countless hours of the wedding and the special after ceremony footages, I vowed then that I was going to be a lady like Princess Diana; get married to a white Prince in shiny armor, and wear a ring like hers: a stunning oval sapphire surrounded by white round stone diamonds set in platinum. But instead I got knocked up right after high school and the only white Prince I got was a white boyfriend with an 8-mile trucker mouth and a shiny fist of abuse loaded with a Russian Roulette temper. Well I guess I kissed the wrong damn frog!

Determined to pick myself up and dust off that miserable life, I found myself being the top salesperson in the US for six consecutive months of a huge franchised car dealership making over $100,000 in the late '80s. Do you know how much money that was in the '80s? A lot of damn money and I bought everything shiny; a house, 2 brand new cars off the showroom floor, a horse for my son, and I had plenty of jewels to look like a rock star all the time. But with that kind of money, it came with a price tag. I was never home. I was now a used car manager, kicking ass all over the DMV (DC, MD & VA) area, but it meant never being home. I worked open to close almost six days a week. Being away from home took its toll on my marriage. I never saw my kids much and when I did finally get a chance to go home and spend some time with my family, my soon to be psychotic ex-husband managed to accuse me of sleeping with every salesperson in the dealership, just because I was simply always working. He had no idea what it took for a black woman in her mid-twenties to run a car dealership. I don't know what he thought was paying for the house, the cars, the horse, and all the luxuries we had. Eventually I just grew tired of the 60-hour work weeks and coming home to craziness. I soon walked away from that marriage with nothing more than a child support order and my George Foreman Grill. But what I didn't know was that this man would become my "Sleeping with the Enemy" stalker for ten long years. I was free from a marriage of hostility and violence, yet my soul was still in chains; not to mention that because he was a white man, the law did nothing to stop him.

So, what did this beautiful skinny little girl from Washington, DC do to keep her head up through all that traumatic drama? I bobbed and weaved…lol. What that means in Ebonics is that I moved around a lot and hid in many places never giving my address out to anyone until I got tired of hiding and decided to call my grandmother for help. My grandmother whom had lived in Southeast, Washington, DC her whole life, decided to help me by putting an apartment in her name so I could not be found if someone was searching for me. I had found me this cute little apartment in between the Washington DC and Maryland line where it was the worst area to live. I mean if you have seen the movie "Training Day" with Denzel Washington and the neighborhood, he was rolling in: Yep, that was where I lived. The building had one way in and one way out. It was a real New Jack City apartment building. Dealing drugs all day and all night, and lookout boys everywhere was the norm. But it was in the hood, it was $400 a month, and it kept me safe from a crazy white boy that was stalking me. The one thing I knew was that he would not be coming over there without getting shot. No Sir! The only thing white moving over there was a mouse or a cop. Hell, now that I think about it, maybe I should have invited him over. So that building was safe for me in many ways. It was a far way away from the style of living I was used to, but the key word is that I had peace and I was no longer with a man that was physical, emotional and mentally abusive, for no freaking reason.

I mean really: I went from a house in the suburbs with two new cars, a six-figure income job, and a horse, to a drug infested neighborhood. But I was free, and I felt free except for missing my boys which I had to go see on a different turf. But the interesting thing about where I lived, everybody partied, and I found me a new spot to get in trouble. The "Oak Tree" it was the hottest nightclub in town, and I found myself being a regular customer every Thursday, Friday, and Saturday night. It was the joint. Any celebrity in town, that's where they hung out, any gangsters or drug dealers in town, that is where it went down, and then there was me, the light as a feather Dark n Lovely, sexy and sassy Chocolate sister on the prowl. I was such a regular that if I didn't know you, you didn't exist. You fuck with me in "that" club, you got an exit that you didn't see coming. I knew every dude, every celebrity, and every wannabe. Thus, is how I ended up in bed with a famous BET comic that turned me into a twenty-dollar hoe in the wee hours of the morning. Honestly, there are so many famous people, that are A-listers now that I ran amuck with back in the day, but due to their fame, my lips are sealed. But if those walls could talk, eww child my vagina quivers just thinking about it.

Anyway, living in that crazy building and going to that nightclub three nights a week had its ups and downs, it grew me up, and I saw a lot of strange things. Not to mention I met some bodylicious male strippers that turned me on to a new game. I became great friends with a male stripper name "DEEP STROKE", and he invited me to come to his stripper set to see him strip. And just as any lady would do, I went to see him, and his boys do what they do best at the strip club. It was cool and sexually arousing to see them on stage and then to go visit them backstage after their set. It intrigued me, but more importantly, I got to see first-hand how this was more than dancing to them. It was a form of art, and it was their livelihood. These male exotic dancers had kids, wives, girlfriends and families to support. Although the women in the audience were screaming and throwing money, and being rubbed upon in erotic formation, these male dancers were seriously earning their money to take care of home. As my friendship grew with DEEP STROKE, he came to my apartment one night to talk to me about him and his girlfriend. He came to let me know that he was going through some issues with his girl…ding ding ding, ya know what that means, either he coming to your place for a booty call, or he genuinely needs to talk. It was at that moment when I am staring at him in my apartment as he is talking to me about his problems, but I can't hear him because my Va-JJ is talking to me extremely loudly, I mean loud! As he continued to talk, I just said yes. He said cool, I'll be back tomorrow with some things. He then kissed me, hugged me tight and ran out the door. I'm like what, what just happened, did I…did I just tell this guy he could move in? Yes, I did! That was the first time I should have payed attention. But that monstrous creature of a vagina, took a message of its own.

Now you would think with a male stripper starting to hang around your apartment with you, you would be having mad sex. But that wasn't the case, in fact he was still in love with his girlfriend. I think he just needed a cool down period to gather his thoughts. And if you know me, oh baby gather those thoughts over here, I want to see your mind work. What? Don't judge me! Lol.

As he started hanging around the apartment more often, I got the chance to see him prepare for his set. Now ladies, if you ever get a chance to see a man get ready for a stripper set, that includes; taking a shower, then drying off and rubbing baby oil all over his body while his Mandingo is hanging, let me tell you, your vagina will do some jumping jacks at a speed you never felt before. All I could say to him was: "Boy don't come over here and ask me to oil your back; stop playing with my emotions got damn it"! He was brown skin with a body built like a King and I wanted to be the Coke bottle sitting on those fine ass abs. But he never saw me in that light. He was truly focused on getting his girlfriend back and making that money. So, I eventually had to respect his hustle and stop drooling. Grrr… it was tough, I am not going to lie.

One day as I was folding some clothes on the bed he came out the shower naked and started talking to me about his situation and as I dared to turn my head to look at him naked, he asked me: "Why don't you dance"? I said: "I would rather watch you guys dance". But in the back of mine I was saying to myself: "Why the freak not"? But the other part of my brain was saying, I'm due in court soon, I am still fighting psycho for custody of my sons, and I got friends, what if they see me, what If someone tells, but I do need the money and I am good looking with a nice body, and I am sort of free. But I said no. I wasn't ready for that life, at least not now. But I said to myself if he ever asks again; fuck it, I am doing it. Guess What? About a week later as we were in the car headed to the strip club, he asked. And just like that I became "Dark & Lovely" a female stripper on the down-low.

The rules were not on this side of town, so we crossed the tracks, that means going to a different hood. We crossed the tracks (railroad) pass the Navy Yard in Washington, DC, far away from the clubs on my side of town. I was always a good dancer anyway, so this couldn't be that much harder right? Think again! Understanding your body parts and understanding how to work them in motions you never felt before or seen before is an understatement. And if you don't feel sexy or confident about your body then forget about it. Luckily, I was still a small framed little chocolate girl that had smooth skin, pretty face, pretty smile and I had some boobs. I never had an ass though; God just didn't give me one. I am probably the only black girl in America that is still looking for her ass. But my big boobs compensated for that. In no time I had my sexy wearable gear (costume) and the sexy slow songs were easy to work your body to. Then all you needed were a few drinks to warm your body and soul, and you just work your body to the music with a routine. It wasn't hard to do. It was a mind getaway, it was fun, I had my stripper brothers in the house, so I didn't have to worry about no crazy shit popping off. But one day I went to the strip club with DEEP STROKE and I watched a guy I had never seen on the stage before and he took my breath away. He had me at a low…real low, and I tried hard in writing this book not to mention "real" stage names, but his name was "Good n' Plenty". As I say, I normally don't mention "real" stage names, but seeing as this was over 25 years ago, I think, it's ok. Because I did hear that name at another club, so guessing which one it was…be my guess. Lol. Believe me when I say: "If My Vagina Could Talk". He gives the candy called "Good n' Plenty" a whole new meaning. Fuck a whole new Genre. It didn't take me long to get that introduction and before you could say Va-JJ I fell hook, line and sinker in lust with him. When he invited me back to his place I thought, ok this will just be a quickie, sex is sex, what the hell, let's do this.

    He had a big beautiful bed that had shear white soft flowing curtains hanging from the ceiling that draped all over the canopy bed. It was the sexiest thing I had ever seen. That alone had me moaning before he touched me. He put on music as if this was not his first time at the rodeo and I am a sucker for slow sexy music with erotic lyrics. Then I hear Keith Sweat singing and he begins to dance on top of my body as if he was on stage. At this point, who needs penetration…good lawd, I am losing my mind already. As he moves closer to my body, my anxiety and my Va-JJ are having a Black Snake Moan moment that has my body completely chained to him. As I slowly look up at these beautiful sheer curtains that he has now wrapped my legs in, all I could think about was submission and the thought of me not being able to control my body because I was tied up sexually in these beautiful sheer curtains and I couldn't move. Thank goodness I had a little figure back then barely 110 lbs., because if you were to wrap my legs up in some shit like that today; the whole ceiling coming down; Code 10 girl down, call 911.

After I started to feel the penetration and started to slowly move my body in sync with his, he said softly: "Don't move". He then started to wrap my arms in the sheer curtain and press on my hands to hold me down and he said it again: "Don't move". Let me tell you at this point "50 Shades of Gray" ain't shit. This young man was more than "Good n' Plenty", that name did not do him justice. He cradled my body in formations I didn't know I could do, and the beats from the music playing, I felt every beat in his muscles. He had mastered the art of seduction on and off the stage. I couldn't feel my legs, and then I noticed we were no longer on the bed, I remembered my head hanging off the bed, but I don't remember how we got to the floor. He was total domination! For his grand finale, he unwrapped me and just when I thought he was done, he sexually jumped on me as I had seen him do on stage. It was that moment believe it or not I had my first orgasm and I completely froze. And the best part, he didn't lean over me and hand me a twenty-dollar bill or call me a cab; he kissed my body gently and laid on his back and he asked the question in a sexy tone as he patted my thigh: "You Good". Now, how the hell do you answer that question when your body is still numb, your brain has left the building and a tear is waiting to drop from the corner of your fucking eye because it was that damn good. I took a deep breath and turned my face to the opposite side of him so that, that one little freaking tear could fucking fall out of the corner of my eye without him noticing. And when it finally fell, I put my hand on his thigh and said: "Yea, I'm good".

I know you must be wondering why I remember it so vividly as if it was yesterday, because it was the best sex I have ever had to date. You don't forget that kind of sex no matter how old you get. I think the best part of him was that he was not a big tall guy with this humongous penis. He was a medium framed guy, but he was just solid and confident about his shit. He had mastered making love or having sex, whichever coin you toss. Can you even imagine being able to have an orgasm without having to move an inch of your body? I didn't see him much after that because the dancing for me ended as quickly as it started, especially as the court date got closer for my kids. Just didn't want to take any chances. So, there was nothing else to do but to go back to the main club and start hanging out again where dancing and drinking was the thing to do.

I thought I had seen the last of Good n' Plenty until one day on the Fourth of July, I was just feeling like I needed something, not sure if it was sex or just simply a male companion, so I did the unthinkable no girl should ever do. I called him! Yes Sir, I excused myself from a family BBQ and went inside and made that phone call. You know the one where you call a guy begging and say: "Hey you remember me"?

And he replied: "Of course I do Ms. Dark n' Lovely, where you been"? I answered in a cute voice: "Looking for you". By now my body is saying what I want it to say. I preceded to tell him that I wanted to be with him now, and he informed me that he was with his girlfriend and her family at a BBQ. But I didn't care, I was living this insane single life, so I wanted what I wanted. I managed to talk him into sneaking out the house to meet me. He agreed and before I knew it, I was parked behind the back of a 7 Eleven waiting for him. Just as I was about to leave thinking he couldn't get away; I look up at the apartment building and I see him climbing out of the second-floor window and he just jumped down. He said that was the only way to get out without getting noticed because if he had gone out the front door, everyone would have noticed.

We zoomed away to another area and had mad crazy sex in the back of my Ford Escort. It was just as liberating as it was before. The exhale was well worth the deep breath. But just like that, that was the last time I ever saw Good n' Plenty. Gone but never forgotten!

Even though I was living this free almost single life, my life was a pretty mess. I was still this young beautiful black sister in "Chocolate City" running from a stalker and a white man at that. How the hell did this happen, it was like I blinked, and my world went to shit. Working a normal 9-5 job, fighting for a divorce and custody of my children while clubbing three nights a week just to take the edge off the insanity while hoping and praying for an end to it all, just seemed like a nightmare dream I just could not wake up from. I just wanted to live like a normal person, with not even knowing what the hell normal was. All I knew was that I was doing it alone, no one to talk to and no one to help me dodge all these bullets coming at me just because I had enough of the marriage, I had enough of the mental abuse, I had enough of not feeling worthy. I just knew I was way too young to endure such mental pain. To make matters worse, did I not get the memo; I got married at the Virginia Court House by a Justice of the Peace Officer during my lunch hour and went back to work. Talk about a shotgun wedding, who gets married during lunch hour? How the hell did I not see that freaking bright ass red flag. They were flashing and tooting horns, and I was so freaking ignorant to the obvious. What a pretty mess that was!

It was like I went from this strict Jehovah's Witness home where I ran away every chance I got to this mental and physical abusive trapped marriage at the age of 20, and then to this life of just running the streets for freedom. I went from a teen mom to a married woman by the age of 20. Why did I get married, I felt, it was the right thing to do to raise a child? What the hell did I know, I sure screwed that up. I never loved him and was never in love and the sex was boring, but the escape from my parent's home made this a haven. Now, let's clarify this, we received whooping's as children as most kids did when you act up, and I got plenty, I was always rebelling. But the worst part of growing up in my household was being subjected to the mental cult of living by the Jehovah's Witness lifestyle and rules. That alone was brain damage on its own, which I never knew how much it had affected my life until after I moved out of my parent's home at the age of 17 and a half. It not only ruined a huge part of my life but, my other siblings and family members as well. You would think a connection to God through religion is supposed to be peaceful. Well you didn't hear it from me or maybe you did, I would rather run butt naked in a pit of snakes and take my chance at survival than being raised in the Jehovah's Witness cult.

The partying life was my escape to fulfill my lonely nights and discomfort of not feeling worthy enough as a mom or as a woman. It was just so darn hard to be young, beautiful and smart when you were alone. Nobody wanted to hear your story, nobody wanted to understand, and nobody wanted to take sides for fear of their safety. So, I became this dark loner with a fulfilling night life to ease the pain. Some people do drugs, smoke, drink or even cut themselves to ease away the pain, but for me, the sound of music in a crowded night club with a few shots of tequila and some dancing, was my fix. It was the obsession of the oppression.

I remember when the dating game with men became a must. I think I was trying to find a replacement for what I thought I had or thought I wanted, but it was just sex and a part-time companionship. But I must tell you, it was fun, and I met some great guys and some bad guys along the way. In all fairness I have to say living in a "Nino Brown" type building turned out to be cool and a great haven for me. My next-door neighbor James and I became awesome friends. When I saw him at the club one night as he tried to pick me up, when I turned around, we noticed that we were neighbors, so the friendship took off in an awesome way. He had my back when I had men over, I had his when he had women over. We had a signal for trouble or for help. We would knock on the wall, or perhaps excuse ourselves and knock on the door. It was the funniest thing, especially when I could hear him having sex and his bed was next to my living room wall, the whole wall would shake, and he would be pounding. I never knew if it was a knock for help or he was taking a girl to New York. You see James was a New Yorker. He was a smooth handsome dude from New York that always dressed to the nines. It didn't matter what he wore, which was usually African attire, he made it all look good and he smelled heavenly. James had this big beautiful canvas of the city of New York behind his bed that lit up his bedroom. It was a beautiful piece of art hanging right over his bed. He used to tell me, when he had girls over, he enjoyed taking them to New York, so if I heard the walls knocking against my wall, not to worry, he's going to New York. It was the funniest thing. That was my signal he had company, and he had company often...lol. So, it became this running joke between he and me when we were at the club together. I could tell by watching him in the club with women, who was going to be the next girl going to New York, no airline or bus ticket required. LOL!

I remember one crazy night after my best friend, and I left the club and came back to my place just a little intoxicated and James heard us come in. Let me tell you, that man could smell fresh meat a mile away. Shortly after we arrived, here comes that all too familiar knock at the door. It was my best friends first time meeting him, so I introduced James to her. He looked at her as if she was a biscuit on a hot plate of jelly. And for some odd reason, she returned the same look. The next thing I know she went to New York, oh and the hard part was I had to hear it. When she comes back to my apartment, we were silent and then I just had to say it: "So how about Manhattan, nice huh"! She looked at me and I looked at her with this grin, and all we could do was bust out laughing. It was straight comedy; we both knew what going to Manhattan meant. This was a strong "fight the power" Black Panther type of brother from New York. He was strong in everything he did.

That was my life for a few years; working, partying, sharing my boys on weekends, while continuously being stalked by psycho. I finally decided to move out of this building and cross the bridge to Virginia. I wanted to be a whole State away from this idiot. This lasted one whole month, until my soon to be ex-husband broke into my apartment and tried to kill me. Luckily my neighbors ran to help me. I fled the scene not remembering I was in the middle of cooking because

I was about to entertain a male dancer and his friend whom was on their way over to have dinner with me in my new apartment. Two brothers with bodies built like a Greek God were on their way to my house for dinner (that's my story and I am sticking to it). Luckily the scene was over before they got there because how tragic would that of been a white man choking me half to death and two black dudes walk in. I think we all pretty much know how that story would have ended.

After that frightening event, I decided to leave the State until the courts could put this insane man in some type of either a 5150 hold or lock him up. But domestic violence in those days, just got slaps on the wrist. What the hell is that? Could it have been because I was a young black girl and he was a white man, who the hell knows, but one thing for sure was I needed a windfall break from it all.

One drop kick later to the gut, I found myself in Atlanta at my parents' home to escape Mr. Psycho from hell and to simply breathe for a moment. Perhaps I was looking for something new or perhaps a fresh start. But the only problem was my parents were Jehovah's Witnesses and I was the "bad seed" or the child from hell that got pregnant at 18. So, I knew I couldn't stay in their home long before the "go to the Kingdom Hall" would be an anthem I would wake up to everyday.

My memories of being a Jehovah's Witness was just pure hell for me. It was like I had fallen from Grace in my parents' eyes especially after I had been disfellowshipped from my family and congregation at the very young age of sixteen. After that I vowed never to step foot in a Kingdom Hall for the rest of my life. The memories of being court-martialed to a meeting where five white Elders of the congregation and one black Elder sat behind this long table with the verdict of guilty on their faces as my dad, my mom, and I walked into the room. It was the most chilling thing I had ever experienced. Can you imagine a fragile little black girl, barely 90lbs soak and wet, walking into a dark room with her parents to sit in front of them in those cold metal folding chairs, waiting to learn your fate? It was like I was being taken to eat my last meal. And to think, I was being court-martialed because I went to a slumber party where there were no parents at home, and someone said I was smoking a cigarette at the slumber party. So, this is my fate? I am being court-martialed over smoking a cigarette at sixteen years old. Ya gotta being kidding right?

Before I knew it, this cute little chocolate girl had the firing squad firing questions at her about that night of an unsupervised slumber party. But there was one thing as scared as I was, I knew not to do and that was not to snitch. When you are born and raised in the hood, you don't snitch, it's the code of honor badge you wear for life! I sat there and never spoke for over an hour, and according to them not only did I refuse to speak or look up at them as they fired all these questions at me, I refused to snitch on the other girls or tell them what really happened that night. No Sir! Fuck You! You get nothing! So, it left them no choice but to disassociate me from the congregation and my family. No one could no longer communicate with me and that includes my siblings, my parents, and anyone at the Kingdom Hall. And to make matters worse, I was forced to go to the congregation the following day, where I sat as they announced my name along with the other girls that attended the party. As they read the names in front of the entire congregation to tell them we had shamed the organization, I was the only one, yes me this little black girl that was fully excommunicated. The other girls which were all white, were not excommunicated. Do you know how embarrassing and how horrible I felt, not to mention the embarrassment my family must have felt. It was like being stoned in public. But the interesting thing about this story which, I never told anyone until now, right now in writing this book, is that I was only the lookout girl at that party. I was the girl that was made to sit on the porch like a porch nigger to look out and make sure no parents were coming. I literally was so scared sitting on that porch outside by myself in the dark, that I called a friend over to come sit with me. He was a high school friend of mines brother, whom I liked but never really got to spend time with, so I invited him over to keep me company as these white girls partied, drank and smoked in the house. His name was Richard. He came and sat with me for hours on the porch as we could hear the noise from inside the house. After a while we started to kiss on the porch which later turned to us going inside, passing the party room and making out. Yep, we had sex, he broke my virginity at the party. That night I lost my virginity to a guy that was 23 years old and I was still in high school. And to think I got court-martialed and shamed for smoking a cigarette and being a look out girl, but I should have been court-martialed for having sex. Is that not the craziest thing ever? But what the hell, I would have lied and denied it anyway. But the funny thing is I don't remember the sex, I remember the semen because it freaked me out, I did not know it had a white color and I thought that was me…lol. Boy was I dumb. I had to ask him: "What the hell is that"? I was just this scared little girl thinking I am protecting the other girls and I got shamed for the wrong thing which unbeknown to me affected most of my adult life. That feeling of being summoned to a jury and already being convicted sent a chill down my spine that affected me for many years of feeling unworthy and not good enough. It took years to shake that feeling, and sometimes I still have that feeling of unworthiness. It is something I will never be able to shake which still causes me anxiety sometimes. I wish I could go back and sue all those fuckers from the trauma they have caused me through life.

So, when I said going to my parents' house to breathe a little was going to be tough, that was the reason. Those freaking memories still haunt me. But, hiding out in Atlanta started to take its toll on me because I knew no one and I was severely missing my sons and becoming depressed. But getting away from Washington DC for the moment seemed like the better choice. I used to get in my car on a Friday afternoon and drive 12 hours on the weekend to share the kids and pick them up. Sometimes I used to do a turnaround and bring them all the way back to Atlanta for one day and get up on Sunday and drive them 12 hours back to DC. I was one tired little lady come Monday morning. One Monday morning after that long drive on the road, I just called my amazing attorney and told him, I can't do it anymore and to file the divorce and custody papers immediately, I was completely over it. Kapesh!

Within a few short weeks I found myself getting a job in the jewelry business for this wonderful family that were experts in custom made fine jewelry and diamonds. They became my greatest friends and were like family to me. But one day a famous Football player came in the store to pick up some very expensive watches he had left for repairs. He was a regular customer buying gold jewelry, and diamonds and one day he invited me to a night club; "Club 21", the hottest night Club in Atlanta at the time. Of course, I went and if you have read anything about me thus far, you know I like to party. So within in a blink of an eye, I became a regular at this night club, once again, Thursday to Saturday, you would catch me there three nights a week, flirting, dancing drinking and partying. Hell, you would have thought I was the hat check girl. I met a lot of famous players, hung out with a few and had an affair with one that was on the verge of a divorce. But, one Friday night, I pulled up at the club and I saw a lot of police activity and the club was closed. Right before my eyes my nightlife of partying had ended and the player I was messing with, their team lost for the season and our FWB (friends with benefits) relationship ended. So hey, my life was starting to spiral again, what do I do now.

Then one day I get this call from an ex-lover from the night club I frequented at in Washington, DC. Not sure how he tracked me down but, he told me he had moved to Chicago and heard I was in Atlanta and asked if he could visit me. I wasn't really trying to be with anyone, not alone fly a man down to see me, and then again men were not on my radar anymore. But against my better judgement, I mentioned to him that I was going to Pensacola, Florida for an all-expenses paid wedding and suggested that he meets me there. Honestly, at that moment I just knew he was going to say "No", but fuck, he said: "Yes". Then I was like Fuck, what do I do now? I can't take it back. So, on the plane I flew. But first, let me tell you this was a wedding of all weddings. I was invited by my co-worker who was the bride. Her family was very wealthy, and her dad was a retired decorated military man. He pulled out all the stops for his beautiful daughter. Every guest was treated like royalty for three days leading up to the ceremony to include; free flight, free hotel, all meals, caravan at your disposal to take you around town and to the beaches, hair and makeup if you needed it, all food and liquor at your disposal and an open invitation to all the family parties and events leading up to the wedding day. My friend and I enjoyed this 5-star champagne vacation, and on the night of the wedding after this glorious reception, the father of the bride put us all in about 10 party vans and took us to a night club that he had paid for the entire night just for guest. I mean really who rents out an entire nightclub just for the wedding reception after party. This was the first time; I mean the first time I was drunk where I didn't even remember being taken back to the hotel. And that my friends, was the night my third child; my beautiful daughter was conceived. Yep, in Pensacola, Florida in a five-star Hotel.

After that trip, my friend went back to Chicago and I went back to Atlanta, not knowing I had precious cargo in tow. And nope I don't remember if the sex was good or bad, even till today, I just remember partying and waking up to pack my bags, because all the out of town guest was headed to the airport. I think back and remember some intimacy and some throwing up, but that is about it. I was two shits to the wind. Kapesh! Gone!

A few weeks later, I remember calling my attorney and telling him, I am with child and asking him will that hurt me in divorce court. Of course, he said yes, and that I had to keep it a secret till my court appearance, and I did. I never returned to Washington DC, to see my sons, but I flew them into Atlanta several times to visit and they kept my secret. Less than 10 days after having the most horrible c-section with major complications, I found myself driving with my mom to my divorce hearing. Yes, I drove 12 hours in a car with a stick shift, feeling like every stich inside of my body was tearing as I shifted gears for 12 hours, but it was worth it for a divorce. When that judge repeated to me over and over asking me: "Mam are you sure you want nothing: no furniture, no heirlooms, not anything from the divorce settlement"? All I could think of was joint custody and my George Foreman Grill. Yep, it's funny, that was the only three things I wanted: a dissolution of marriage, my sons, and my George Foreman Grill. He could have everything, I mean everything. I did not give a SHIT. Just poof be gone out of my life!

The WEIRD thing is, I remembered a long time ago, my mom said to me: "I would have paid a crack head five dollars to bump him off a long time ago". In return I told her: "Yep I should have but guess what…that same crackhead would have snitched for six dollars".

And just like that I was divorced! Amen, let all the fat ladies sing. I was officially and finally single with joint custody. It was a long time coming, a day I had been dreaming about for many years. And let me be the first to say to these men out here, when you are trying to be a good father and see your kids and you dealing with these bitter bitches, and yes I said it, horribly bitter bitches that keep you from your kids unless you show them some love, or give them some money or continuously sleep with their bitter asses. I feel your pain, and "YES" I am saying it out aloud from the mountain top: Child support **can** be over-rated! These women that use their kids as pawns to get back at the men that planted the seed inside of them to give birth can be stalking horrible people. I despise of any woman or any man that holds the kids as hostage for their own psychotic bitterness. I have lived through that horrible traumatic nightmare, and all I can say to you for encouragement is fight to the death. Fight them assholes forever. All my children suffered from the debacle of a bitter divorce, even a child that wasn't his. When you hold children hostage due to a failing relationship, you kill us all inside.

Fast forwarding to my life after my divorce, I put my daughter and her dad on a plane to Chicago because his brother had committed suicide over a girl that didn't love him back. This was a tragedy for his family. As I stayed back in Atlanta while they were away, I was asked to go out for drinks with a co-worker. While we were out having drinks, my co-worker introduced to a male friend of hers named Alex. Alex was everything, you know when your eyes meet someone, and you can tell his soul. It was the first time; I felt some sort of love at first site. However, I didn't act upon it because he was with another girl on a date at the bar. So, I blew it off as if my Va-JJ was having a moment. Then as most clubbers do when it's last call for alcohol, we left and headed to the International House of Pancakes (IHOP). Once we arrived, I noticed he was alone as we were all standing in line to be seated. So, my friend asked him where his date was. He proudly said: "I told her the night was over, plus I wanted to be with you guys, alone".

It was at that moment, I realized he meant me, and I was feeling the same. We all ate, laughed and had a good time and in the wee hours of the morning we all left and went home. About a week or two later, I was at work and that same friend invited me to a Super Bowl party. I declined, I had so much packing to do because I had already given notice to my job, I was moving to Chicago to reunite with my daughter and her dad. He had already found a place for us and I was about two weeks away from moving there. Then she told me that the guy I had met at the club the other week named Alex, it was his party and he sent me a special invitation to come. Hmmm, if you know me by now, you know I am going, I got no loyalty to anyone at this point in my life. So, of course I went, not knowing that this was a complete set up from Alex and my friend. At his Super Bowl Party, I was the center of his attraction and affection. He never left my side all night. He had silently fell in love with me, without barely knowing me. Apparently, he had been trying to get to me for a few weeks. Well, I was smitten, and I never went back home that night. After the guest left, we talked for hours on his waterbed about life, women, men, children and where we both were in life and what we wanted in life. Turns out he went through some of the same pain with an ex-wife.

I had to tell him. I told him I am already packed and leaving for Chicago in two weeks. This thing, this thing called relationship, is never going to happen, I am about to leave Atlanta for good. He looked at me and said: "Well if I only got two weeks, then let's make this the best damn two weeks of our lives". It was something like writing a

Hollywood movie script. And when I tell you he gave me the best two weeks of my life…it started that night. We made passionate love on the waterbed where we put three holes in the bed that night. We had to stop making love to put duct tape on the bed. That was funny. We were wet and water was leaking but we continued to make passionate love.

    I lived with this man for two weeks and I was mentally refusing to go to Chicago. He gave me everything a girl ever wanted. For the first time in my life I had fallen in love. I had met his son and was becoming a part of his life. The deadline had come and passed, and I had not left for Chicago yet. My mother called me to ask me: "Linda, what are you doing"? I didn't have an answer. All I knew was that I met this loving and caring sole that was loving on me to the utmost. Something I had never felt before. It was a genuine connection of unconditional love and I had honestly decided in my mind to stay in Atlanta with him. And then I decided to make that dreadful call to my daughter's dad to tell him I am not coming, but I will fly in to pick up my daughter and bring her back. But before I made that call, Alex came home that night and we had this long awaiting conversation about my choice. As I began to talk, he interrupted me and said: "Go". He told me that I should finish what I started so that I would never have any regrets in life. He said if our love was meant to be, I would be back, and he would wait for me. The following week he took me to dinner, so I thought, but he had secretly planned a surprise going away party for me at a night club. To think this man loved me enough, knowing I was leaving to go to another man, to send me away with a bang. No regrets! He wanted to finish our lives together on a high note knowing I was loved and that he would always be there for me for life. You cannot get much better than that from a man.

As I left to leave for Chicago, Alex and his best friend came to send me off. He bought along his best friend Rueben. Rueben and I never really got along. Rueben was a womanizer and an OG (which means Original Gangster) from the streets of Inglewood, California. He had a pretty scandalous reputation to include smacking a few women around here and there. So, we always bumped heads when all of us would meet up and I never liked the women he would bring on the double dates with us. But for some reason, Reuben didn't tussle with me too much. I think he knew I was a vocal firecracker and he didn't want to catch my wrath. Nevertheless, he was the best friend of the man I loved so I tolerated his bullshit. So off I go leaving my 1965 mustang in the hands of Alex as a parting gift. I knew the goodbye was going to be hard, but I got through it and moved to Chicago.

Everything was set up for me in Chicago. My daughter was treated like a queen by her grandparents and even had a nanny. I had a beautiful place to live, I was given a car and I found a job right away. It seemed like life was good; my daughter was going to Roycemore Academy which was a top-rated private school in Evanston, IL and I was meeting people and making good friends. However, as the years went by, I kept in touch with Alex weekly, we had long talks and discussed our lives. Was that cheating? I don't know, but our friendship never died. He accepted my move but, in his heart, he was still waiting for me.

Almost five years later, on the date of my birthday, I got a call from Alex. He told me he had met someone and that he needed to know if I was ever coming back. I cried like a baby. Everything inside of me told me to pack my bags and run, but the reality was, I had a great job, my daughter had just signed to the top Modeling Agency in Chicago and she was in high demand. I thought long and hard because I had built a new life in Chicago. But I had to go with my heart, and I told him now was not a good time for me to leave and it wasn't about my daughters father because our relationship had deteriorated years before, it was simply the fact that I was finally stable. No clubs, no partying, I had achieved my Associates Degree, and my life was finally on the best path it had ever been, even with my sons. Not to mention, that I had somehow stumbled upon gambling at a local casino and was high rolling on a mistaken identity, well not totally a mistaken ID. I was getting a huge kickback for someone to be me. The money was awesome, and I was finally getting ahead, and as a single mom having bills to pay, you do what you gotta do. So, I declined to leave Chicago. It was a bittersweet ending but, I gave him my blessings to marry this woman; and he did. WOW... he waited five years!

Now here is the funny thing about life: less than six months after I said no to a man I dearly loved, my daughter's dad and I were completely over. When you talk about "No Regrets", I wish I could have gotten that phone call again. Yes, Alex was the one that got away. Huge Regret! BIG MISTAKE!

Nevertheless, many years later, my daughters career started to excel, and we moved to Hollywood for TV and Film. I had been single now for quite a few years and sexless. It was just not a priority. Raising my kids and focusing on my career had taken a huge presence. Little did I know, Hollywood was the most expensive place I had ever lived, and the lifestyle was like going to another country. I had never seen the glitz, the glam, the fakeness, the outlandish personalities and so many backstabbers in my life. It was not the norm. Everybody had an agent, everybody had a manager according to them and everybody said: "Let's do lunch", which really meant SCREW you...I am not that interested. The hate from people daily was just horrid. One thought, how the hell do you survive in this town.

But coming from Washington, DC, and surviving a serial stalker, I figured I got this. I decided to take California by the balls like a street fight in my old neighborhood and just squeeze the shit out of it until it either broke me or I broke the hate against me for trying. Well it broke me more than once, in fact it led my daughter and I to homelessness twice, but that's a whole other book...lol. But my daughter and I held on through determination and we started to turn it around. In fact, the beginning of our turn around moment was after my daughter appeared on two different television shows. We started to understand the work, and we started to understand the industry and the artistry, and what it meant to knock on the doors of the key decision makers. But honestly, I think the defining moment for us was when we met these two amazing A-list actors. The first one was Terrance Howard and it was right after Hustle & Flow became a huge hit. Meeting Terrance Howard at a SAG (Screen Actors Guild) event and talking to him, gave us both a better respect for the art. What he told us both changed the way we looked at Hollywood. He gave us the courage and strength to take charge of my daughters' career during that time. Shortly after, we met Taraji P. Henson also at a SAG event, and knowing that she was from my hometown, the questions were endless and her encouragement to continue was well received by the both us.

We focused our energy on so much more than just running and spinning our wheels on cattle calls and pointless auditions. It took some time, but we made it work for us and I could breathe a litter easier living in that town.

As the years passed by, things got better for us, we met so many people that became our family, we fell deep into the young Hollywood celebrity status with many red-carpet events, parties, productions and more. And along the way I still maintained my long-distance monogamous relationship with Alex over the phone even visiting him in Atlanta twice when I went to go see my mom. Keeping it strictly a great friendship was perfect for us. I was afraid to love again, I was afraid to mingle in Hollywood, I pretty much just didn't want to go through the motions. I compared a lot of guys to him and never really gave them a fair shot. I missed that kind and gentle manhood and that cuddling voice in my ear. The California men were just from Mars. They were all pretty Ricky's trying to be a star, and if you were not giving them a part in your next film or production, they pretty much kicked you to the curb. In reality let's call it what it is, they were full of shit. It was all about them. Have you ever been to a town where the men are maintained and prettier than you? No? Well book a ticket to Hollywood! Well my poor little Va-JJ had shriveled up. It had no interest in anybody I secretly dated, none of them sparked my fire in California, in fact they all bored me to death. I never knew if they were real or fake. There was always a hidden agenda with them.

Just as I was about to give up on men, I get this call from Alex. I remember because it was about a year after my middle son had passed away. I answered the phone and he was calling to tell me Reuben was in town in California. Yep, you guessed it, his crazy ass best friend that I always bumped heads with when we were in Chicago. Alex gives me his phone number and tells me to meet up with him and say hello. I was like why the hell would I talk to him he is crazy as hell. So, I didn't call him, but he called me, with that crazy ass OG tone. I must admit, it was kind of nice to hear an old friend from the past just to shoot the breeze with. Reuben explained to me that his dad was sick and that he came back to California to be with his dad. That pulled some strings in my heart, so I agreed to have dinner with him. A week or so later we met at an IHOP near my house and we talked and laughed for hours over pancakes just reminiscing about the old days of clubbing and hanging out in Atlanta. Okay… don't ask me how it happened but we winded up making out in the backseat of my car. Yep my Va-JJ was finally alive again…lol. Blame it on Aunt Jemima pancakes or the syrup, toss a coin or say what you want, but it happened. I mean really let's analyze this, I just slept with my ex-lover's best friend, and I am still in love with my ex-lover. How the hell does that happen? Yikes, only to my crazy ass could this happen. I tried to blame it on Va-JJ, you know she has a mind of her own, and I have no clue who unleashed that monstrous creature that night. Maybe I was sexually frustrated or maybe I was just tired of being lonely. It was like my Va-JJ was screaming let me out of prison. Nope, none of that justification works for me. Let me be honest with myself and my readers, I wanted to know what that OG had, all that talking shit when we used to all go out together, so wassup, what you got. There I said it! What the hell, yes, I was wrong, but got damn it, Alex was married so … oh well! It wasn't like I was ever going to be with Alex again, and besides it had been more than ten years since I had any type of intimacy with Alex. Hey, I justified it in my mind and that's the end of that. I am sticking to my story.

Reuben and I had started the sparkles to a flame without knowing it, but we both knew one of us had to tell Alex that we were now in a relationship. We thought about it and then we didn't. Until one night he came over and after having sex, I mean immediately after my phone rang and it was Alex on the phone. Just asking if I had ever hooked up with his homeboy Reuben. We both stared at the phone speechless and became silent. It was like the world stopped and we were lying next to each other in bed. I just said to myself fuck it, tell him. So, when he asked me again, I said: "Yes, I hooked up with him and he's right here". In that moment, my entire body went numb. All I could do was hand Reuben the phone and wait for the bomb to drop. Why I felt like I was cheating on a married man, I don't know. I felt like my beautiful friendship with him was over. Kapesh! I was wrong, dead wrong. Reuben handed the phone back over to me and Alex asked me to put him on speaker phone and I did. He joked for a moment about the two of us that always hated each other hooking up. He said when I said he was right here, all he could say was got damnit, Reuben you than stole my girl. But he said it in a joking way and then said: "Honey, you are my best friend. I would rather see you with him than anyone else. You have my blessing. I love him he's my best friend and I love you. You too are some crazy people and I'm happy for you both". When talking about that going well, it's an understatement. Ladies, when I tell you, that man was the one that got away. I never lied. He will always have my heart on a silver platter. Alex was still just as amazing as the day I met him.

Reuben and I became so close that I started to love him dearly. He eventually moved in with me as we were contemplating marriage. My kids liked him, and he was just a joyous guy to have around and being an OG had its brownie points because he protected us in many ways. I had been knowing him and his ways for over 12 years. Sex was great with him, and when we fussed, the makeup sex was even better. He loved me unconditionally and we were doing well…or were we. It was that call that ended it all. What call do you dare ask me? The call when a man calls you and say, I am not coming home tonight. You know if I had not known his previous past of being a womanizer, I may have been a little more shocked that he was creeping. But I knew him and his past all too well. He was a playa (someone who plays the field or has prowess in gaining romantic and sexual relationships). And more importantly, so was I. But I thought we both agreed when he moved in that would all stop. But hey, apparently, he didn't get the memo so, I felt it was my duty to read it to him. I simply told him in a nice tone:

"Dude, first, of all you can't out play a playa. Next, if you not laying your head on my pillow tonight, you are laying it on somebody else's. And lastly, you got about 45 minutes to come get yo shit"! Now of course he threatened me with that OG shit. My response was; boy bye. I hung up and immediately called Alex and told him to tell his best friend to hurry up and come get his shit. Alex just laughed. He then reminded me that regardless we all have been friends for many years, and not to go ham, both of us played each other so let it go. And just like that it was seamless, and our intimate relationship was over. Kapesh! No regrets!

The crazy thing about this triangle of friendship for 25 years, the three of us are still the three Amigos. We are still in each other's lives with respect and love one another. I still love these two guys with my whole heart. We are still inseparable. Sometimes we do three-way calls, and I can call them for anything right now in this very moment. I have been in this triangle of love for a long time and I seriously don't know if it will ever change. It's just a bond I cannot describe, and most will never understand, and I could give a flying fuck. Those are my boys for life!

A few months after Reuben and I split up, but maintained a great friendship, I was diagnosed with severe vaginal bleeding and I had been losing a lot of blood, not to mention early cancer signs, so my beautiful black female doctor (which I had to mention all that about her because it is extremely hard to find a black female gynecologist) and I decided on a full hysterectomy. I was so relieved to do it, and I called my OG Reuben to come take care of me, and he did. He even picked my parents up from the airport and bought them to the hospital. He came to the house and cooked for us every day and became great friends with my mom and dad. And he was the first one to test out the new booty as he called it after my 8-week check-up. He felt he deserved that honor for taking care of me. He was always comedy in his own way.

Shortly after my 8-week checkup I noticed that instead of having my normal menstruation since that was impossible now after a full hysterectomy, I was starting to have sexual tensions during those peak days of the month. It was like, my period went away and was replaced with this sexual beast of an organ that was stronger than my normal sexual arousal. Of course, I asked the good doctor, and she said I was going through a mild hormonal change and she suggested medication. But I am not one to take meds, so I declined. Now ask me if that was a regret. LOL…Hell Yea!

My body had become this one big huge craving machine once a month. But I have learned to tame it and keep that monstrous creature under control. Some months it's an episode scene from the movie "Black Snake Moan" and some months it's ridiculous shopping or gambling (playing poker) does the trick, or I simply keep my black ass home and write a good movie script, watch a bad movie so I can complain about the writing or I simply annoy family and friends on Facebook. Either way you slice it, it comes, and it goes, and I am ready for that sucker. LMAO! My vagina truly talks to me and I listen, I listen well. Don't call me crazy, I just own up to my shit!

I must laugh somedays because I feel like I came thru this furious fire pit since I was a teenager to be now in my mid-fifties and must deal with this hormonal witch that lives deep inside my vaginal walls. She has silence and yet she can be so vocal where she can create this loving crazy person that just wants to be loved for who she is. Some say its anxiety, some say it's crazy, I say its Life!

Now I am living in the enclave of Hollywood with this fiery anxiety and sexual disorder that seems to unravel without warning. Sure, it would have been easy to take the hormonal pills, but how boring that would have been. I am in Hollywood for goodness sakes, we are all a little crazy. I think I fit in perfectly. LOL!

Living in Los Angeles for fifteen years was beautiful. I met the most wonderful friends that are now part of my family. I started a lot of careers and some of those you hear on the radio today and you see in magazines or watch on TV. I was always this hidden secret behind the scenes of many things or involved in crap I had no business dealing with, but I have too many stories to tell, perhaps that will be something I visit in another book, but my time in Los Angeles was starting to come to an end. The cost of living was seriously not justifiable anymore. My glam lifestyle and my free-spirited lifestyle came at a price I didn't want to pay anymore, plus the anxiety and frustration there of just having no work-life balance started to take a toll on me. I wanted more at a lesser price, I wanted to boss up on life and see my fruits.

My next stop after visiting the State a few times was Houston, Texas. Although Hollywood had become my life and I knew I would miss everyone and the beaches and the weather, I just started to think about my purpose in life and what I could possibly do to change my future if I could invest more in me and my dreams if I cut the cost of living expenses in half. Thus, is why I moved. Funny, how you maneuver through life without a plan and life takes on a path of its own. I just simply decided to put my hands on my own steering wheel.

Moving to Texas was cool at first until I realized I am a city girl, and this place is driving me bonkers being so slow paced. Moving from Hollywood to Texas is like being a cheetah and then becoming a snail. I was going into this lonely depression of what the hell is going on here.

I mean watching the stores close at 9pm and there is no place to get anything after that became the death of me. And no one wants to come out the house to do anything and they are in bed by 10pm. Seriously people? What the hell is that about? And don't ask them to make a quick decision...snail roll. Making a decision becomes this GIGANTIC project task, like they need a white board and a power point presentation. WTF is that about? Yes or No, you do, or you don't? How many people do you have to pray with or talk to before you can decide...really?

After about three months of trying to adjust to this new life in Houston, I reacquainted myself with Edward, an old high school friend via Facebook. Thank God we talked at least twice a day for several months. Edward helped me regain my sanity. Don't get me wrong, I was blessed to have moved, but I was lonely as hell; sexually, mentally, emotionally and anything else you would like to add. It was happening. Edward's birthday was coming up and he invited me to fly into town to spend his birthday with him. Well if you know anything about me by now, I hopped on a plane. He said he was paying for the trip, hell "YES" I am coming. I already knew in my mind sex was going to be involved. But we had spent so many months on the phone, I was already emotionally connected to this "friends with benefits" concept.

If you don't know what "friends with benefits" mean, it means you get all the benefits of a relationship like sex, money, etc., but you are in no way to catch feelings for one another. NEVER BREAK THE FRIEND CODE. Be friends, have sex and keep it moving. Kapesh! But do I have to tell you that my crazy ass broke the code and got heartbroken? Yep me the Playa and fallen and couldn't get up...it's funny now, but at the time I wanted to bust his kneecaps.

I spent nine soothing and quiet days with him in his home, relaxing, sexing, talking and just enjoying each other's company. In fact, on his birthday we managed to have sex five times in one day. That was different. Most guys are done for the day after one sexual escapade. Now, cool your heels, it wasn't in a repeat method, we had sex several times throughout the day. Was it good? Of course, and it fed my crazy sexual hormones like I was a crackhead. Now remember at the beginning of my chapter, I mentioned having sex with this famous BET comic that gave me a twenty dollar bill after sex, well nearly twenty five years later, I wake up after having a long night of sex with Edward and I look on the nightstand table and I see his car keys and $200 dollars. My thoughts were what the fuck, I went from $20 dollars to $200 and it took me twenty-five years to get a pay increase. What the hell is that? Am I in the wrong profession? But after I thought about it, he was paying me for my flight and giving me the keys to his whip while I was in town. Whew...I was about to slap myself.

Once I left and returned to Houston, I felt a stronger connection to him, and as I was slowly breaking the freaking code, he had no clue, that is until he told me his ex was moving back in. I mean seriously could my luck with men get any worse. Why I pick these dudes with freaking ex's all over the place is beyond me. It's a never-ending story for me; it's like I have a freaking sign on my forehead that says: "YOUR EX LIVES HERE"! I am always the rebound girl or the "friends with benefits" chick or simply the around the way girl. Wtf...can a sista get a break here?

I was so distraught for days until I called my boys Alex and Rueben. And to the "t" they both told me the exact same thing: "Linda get the fuck over it! You know better. Did you not learn anything from us"? And there you have it...just like that I was over it. They were so right. How are you going to be a playa and get played? Back in the day, I would have hit it and quit it. They told me I was getting soft. That was hilarious to me. Leave it to them to put me back on track. Edward and I are still great friends and still talk every day and besides, I broke the code, he didn't. Our friendship was much more important. These codefendant emotional relationships take on a life of its own. It's a beast!

While clicking my heels and dusting myself off I found myself loitering on Facebook dating app. Who the hell signed me up for that? I have no clue, but these guys kept popping up in my feed and right before the Thanksgiving Holiday, I answered a "like" you know what those are right? This chocolate brother was as dark as me with green eyes. Ok, green eyes, yeah right? I responded fully believing I was being catfished. In fact, I reported his as spam…lol. I had never seen a dark-skinned brother that was handsome as hell with green eyes. So, I am thinking what is wrong with him. Ladies you know a handsome dark chocolate brother with green eyes should never be single. I mean NEVER! Hell, I'll take the bait! I'm diving in. We connected finally through the phone and it was nice. His voice woke up my Va-JJ, I am not going to lie. He was from NY with that NY accent. His brownie points were starting to add up. But let me say this, I am a workaholic, I am up to the early morning hours, I seriously had no room for dating in my life. I am busy not only building my business, but others as well. I started to think, I got no time for this dude, none; so why play.

I have no clue why I continued to talk to him. But I slowly learned that he was an introvert, very shy, and a total home body. I thought well that's cool, opposites can attract right? Then ding…ding…ding…I found out why this delicious chocolate brother is single. There is an ex. WTF not again! There is an ex and kids. At this point, I am batting ZERO! I mean zero with a capital Z.

I just decided to make the best of it, what the hell it's the Holidays, I am in a new city, and besides I am a playa it's in my DNA. So, I leaped and so far, so good. I mean the sex did not start off great, I think it was because our lives were all over the place at the beginning and I don't think he was that comfortable yet and nor was I. But hey, I really didn't care, it was an itch that needed to be scratched from time to time. I mean I am a single woman and we do have our needs. So eventually we had a talk about the sex, and it was exactly what I thought it was, his comfort zone with my extra strong personality and needs. Well after that talk, he became this NY Power Ranger where I remember being soar for an entire week. Well that talk went well, and I paid for it. And the moral to that story is, be careful what you ask for. LOL. Once again, I have managed to secure another male friend and not a relationship. At this point who cares, I have just decided to be hyped on life and enjoy these precious days as they are given to me.

I have been the life of the party at the worst I could be. I have been bruised and burned, but somehow, I'm intact. Sometimes I eff up I mess up, I hit and miss, but that's the beauty of being perfectly incomplete. I am always still working on my masterpiece and you have not seen the best of me yet. I pray every day and I ask the higher power for direction, good health, and peace and happiness for my family and all those I love.

Chapter 2

THE QUEST OF A GYPSY

~Destiny D.

Here I am, right back where my ambitions of wanting more in life began. I would have never believed it if someone would have told me that I would end up in the same small midwestern Hicksville town 31 years later that I grew up in and almost as penny-less as when I left. I thought I would always tell my stories from afar as to how I got out of the North West Indiana Region dodging bullets literally and figuratively and became a successful businesswoman.

You've heard of the tales rags to riches story yes? Well, I would say my journey is more of a rag to a "better off" story with its scathing pendulum still in full swing pushing me onward.

Where the molding of my persona began:

My name is Destiny. Growing up with my 2 sisters and 2 brothers; I guess you can say, I was supposed to be the perfectly blended middle child. But if you leave it to me to tell it, it's true what they say about the middle child being overlooked. The oldest gets the most hardship for parental expectations and responsibilities, the youngest is always considered the baby and can do no wrong, but the siblings in the middle, well, your parents stare at you for a second as they try to remember your name when yelling out to you or pass you bye to say hello. I don't think they ever got my name right.

When I was very young sitting outside on the steps of our home in Gary Indiana "the armpit of America" literally; we were considered by economic standards as the lower class meaning poor, so there wasn't much else to do but day dream, watch tv and play games in the streets and if the people whom lingered in the night caught up to you, then you found yourself in some serious trouble.

As a young child, I loved to just sit and daydream of what I would become when I got older. I wanted to be a dance choreographer, an artist/musician, and travel around the world, but because as kids we were always being shuffled around from sitters to cousins and family members homes, I guess I was just never grounded enough to believe that my dreams and ambition would come true. So, I simply stopped daydreaming and eventually became a non-believer in my own dreams!

Growing up in Indiana, there was a lot of turbulence in our household. It made me feel like there was always somewhere else I needed to be. I was ok to being left alone and unattended. I felt comfort in solitude. My mind raced all the time with information. I seemed to naturally analyze everything I encountered, and wanted to know what, how, and just why things were as they are. I overwhelmed myself with details for no reasons. I couldn't even watch TV like a normal kid without thinking why did they do or say that? It's not funny it's stupid and where do these people come from on TV that look so different then what I see around me? Where do they live, why is their hair blonde or red and eyes green or blue? I needed answers! This type of thinking became normal for me if there is such a thing of normalcy. All I knew is that I wanted answers, and I wanted them now.

Let me share a very small window of my childhood experiences and how it developed my character significantly to this day.

I grew up in Gary Indiana, an all predominately Black, Hispanic, & Puerto Rican neighborhood from the age of 1 to 13 years old. There was a lot of hostile segregation between the races. I didn't understand any of it at the time I was very young. Based on the standards of ethnicity we all were considered minorities, but Gary township at the time was ruled and ran by the Blacks in my stomping grounds of youth. Everything was controlled, from the actual street name that you could walk on by race to get to and from anywhere, to the time of day you could walk on them before the night set in. You did not want to be out after dark, that world became ugly and unsafe. The gangs controlled the streets and the lively hood on them. You were prey and had to learn how to maneuver the streets and shortcuts at a young age. I had been caught on these streets at night a few times and got into some bad situations that almost changed my life more then I want to recall.

One incident was the time when my sister and I were on our way home. We knew it would be dark before we could make it home. We had no choice but to get home and fast. There was no short cut path while riding on a bicycle. I was sitting on the handlebars and she was peddling us very fast, but then it happened; we were seen by four black guys, two per bicycle. At this moment, you got two choices, peddle faster or get dealt with. Our hearts stopped for a minute, but that's all we had was about a minute to escape. Then the chase was on! They chased us while surrounding us from both sides and continued to grab our handlebars to try and knock us off our bike. I was kicking at them and my sister held steady while focused on the bike for control as to not fall. She knew the danger that would be brought upon us if we fell off that bike. She kept yelling: "Get away for us"! along with other fancy street curse words to try & show them we weren't scared even though our heart was beating a mile a minute in fear. She would lean in and whisper in my ear: "Hold on tight…We can't fall"! I knew she was more worried for me then herself. That's what big sisters do right? Those boys were much older in age and they kept calling us names and saying what they would do to us when they caught us. I was maybe around 10 years old and scared shitless. But, somehow, we managed to stay on the bike and get well into our territory "the safety" line. The guys knew they had chased us too far, but they didn't give up and continued to chase us. Then it happened, we lost speed control and our bike hit the curb hard and we flipped. Our whole bodies flew into some huge sharp thorn bushes. I could hear the guys yelling: "Pull them out…Get them"! The guys tried to grab us by our ankles to pull us out, but the thorns were so embedded into our legs and skin that they could not hold onto to us because the thorns were sticking them. They kept cursing and yelling about the thorns pricking them and gave up. It got quiet. I couldn't see nor hear them anymore. My sister said be very quiet and hold still a little longer. We laid in the bushes bleeding for some time wanting to make sure they were really gone. Enough time had passed, we needed to get home fearing now that our mother would be really upset at the time approaching curfew. We crawled out whimpering feeling the pain and overall experience as we walked home. We told our mother we fell off the bike trying to get home by curfew. We didn't want to upset her but the look on her face when she seen our faces, bleeding, and bodies covered in thorns was enough to know she was angry and scared for us. She ran us a hot bath to soften the thorns before removing them for hours with the tweezers. Talk about pain!

My early childhood day to day consisted of getting to and from school safely, taking alleys and side short cuts to avoid being ruffed up by bullies and gang members hassling outsiders. It was a daily fight to stay safe though I often wondered why this was my life.

But one day I made the mistake of taking a shortcut home from school during my elementary year. I think I was in 2nd grade at the time. I went down an alley all happy humming along with my holly hobby tin lunch box in hand, like I was Dorothy from the Wizard of Oz without a care in the world. Man, would I love to have that relic lunch box now. Anyways, I was walking along and heard a mean dog growling, snarling, and then barking ferociously. I was like uh oh! I look over my shoulder to the right and here he came running full force toward me. I ran as fast as I could, but it wasn't fast enough. The dog knocked me down face first on the ground and had ahold of the back of my thigh with his teeth. I was bleeding and yelling for help. The pain grew worse and I kept trying to get the dog off me and swung my lunch box tight to not lose it, but the Shepard dog was big and had its teeth sunk in more as I fought. He dragged and shook me by the thigh of the pants along the alley and I lost consciousness. The next thing I remember was waking up to voices of people around me. People were standing over me, then I felt them picking me up and putting me in a car. The next time I woke up again I was in the hospital while being held down getting multiple needle shots in the belly for rabies. I am sure you can imagine how painful this must have been for me, which is probably why today I'm not a big dog lover. I don't dislike them I just prefer not to have one as a pet ever...lol!

For fun, I played outside with a few neighbor kids and my sisters mainly along the train tracks that we lived next too. We would bring the train track gate arm down, by using a smashed tin can and press it onto the track with enough weight in a certain spot and it would lower the gate arm down, then we would grab on tightly to the gate arm, then someone would remove the tin can from the track and the gate arm would lift us up to a vertical position which was the challenge to not let go or fall before we could get back down. We would repeat this until every kid had a turn. Sometimes, we would have two or three of us hanging on the gate arm at one time. We were so bad that we broke the gate arm on multiple occasions by doing this. Well, after many train dispatcher's had complaints for repairs, the cops turned their attention to our block and started to drive by frequently as part of their watch list to catch us. We had been made; but I'm not going to lie that was some crazy fun. There were times the train would come through and we would get stuck up there for some time before it passed to let us come down again. Thinking of us playing on the tracks today, out parents would be mortified. Thank God nothing ever happened to any of us.

For the most part, I think I did pretty good doing my best to stay out of harm's way as a young girl. I would watch TV or sit on the front porch while I practiced playing my flute and dreamt about being somewhere else to keep away the outside madness. But by age 11 I did my first drug, tried cigarettes, smoked some weed, drank and hung out with Mexican gang members. It seemed impossible to escape this behavior. I had become a product of my own environment. I called it survival mode. I didn't like it at all really, but I felt I had no choice; as having protection felt safer than to not.

It seemed nothing was safe. Even coming home straight from school was not always safe. I remember the time when our uncle from next door comes rushing in our house asking if we were ok? As my middle sister & I sat in front of the TV with a bowl of cereal and my oldest sister in the kitchen making hers, we all said we were ok and continued watching TV thinking; what's his problem? Well unbeknown to us, our uncle while next door looked out his window and noticed a man crawling out of my mother's bedroom window with a few items in hand. We were being robbed and didn't even know it! My uncle tried to keep an eye out for us from time to time when my mother was at work. Thinking of this situation now is scary! Like WOW, that's a real life "What If" type of story right? Was he in there when we came home? And for how long? Whew! We were all ok and thank goodness the robber never came out of the bedroom. I always wondered did he hear us first, the kids, and then dash out thinking a parent came home with us? We'll never know, I guess. I know if we would have caught him in our room thinking he's trying to take the little toys we had, we might of all jumped him lol! Like man...what the hell! Do you know how hard it is for us to have anything around here ha-ha? But all kidding aside, I'm so glad nothing came of it, not even a police report, so I am thankful for that.

Music was the connection to everything in our lives. We listened to Motown, Soul, Jazz Hip Hop, Blues and danced as part of our everyday routine. The streets were alive! Your clothes were a statement. The way you wore your hair and dressed spoke volumes about your personality. Looking sharp and full of style was plentiful. The Jackson family lived a few blocks from us on third street. Yup that's right! But we never saw them or ran into them. I assumed they were always probably practicing and singing inside, while we were happily playing outside. I guess it's safe to say their hard work paid off.

Food was a big deal in our family. When we had birthday parties, which seemed like all the time, the food spread was ridiculous. We ate like kings for being poor when parties were celebrated. Everyone pitched in and bought a few homemade authentic dishes and don't forget the pinata. It was a time of family gatherings for every occasion. We had a lot of cousins. Too many at times, I couldn't keep track of who was who. But one thing was for sure, I always fell asleep before we made it home in the car or on a couch of the house, we were having the party at. You just never knew how long the parties were going to last. It would always start out as a young person's birthday party but then turn into the all adult night party. That's our culture and it is the norm.

My mother worked multiple jobs. She took the train to work as an accounting clerk into Chicago. For 17 years she worked at a Steel Mill Company located in East Chicago, IN. The Jobs in the steel mill were extremely harsh on men and no ballpark for woman in the mid '70s. Her years of employment jobs consisted of office work, safety clerk, then a laborer, and finally as a mobile operator. The Steel Mills working conditions and environment were reported to be a very dirty grimy labor intense job, while its daily chemical toxic discharge of pollutants of metal, lead, coke and other by-products dispersed into the land, water and the atmosphere as part of building steel for America. I feel even with the EPA working to strive for more stringent emission regulation reduction for public safety, there is still a nuisance of its disposal waste that is not being scrutinized as it should be to date in my opinion. My Mother did the best she could with the turmoil's she endured with raising four children after the father of her first three children left her, with the youngest child being the age of one and the death of her first husband with her fourth child whom was the age of four during our residence in Gary, Indiana.

I was taught both Spanish and English language at an infant age but was spoken to in Spanish mostly in our home from the age of one to five. For my preschool and 1st year of elementary, I had to go to a special charter school for an hour a day prior to my regular school to be taught how to speak proper English. Ironically now at my age my

Spanish is lame for speaking fluently. It's pretty embarrassing being around people who talk fluent Spanish because I now talk what we joke about as "Spanglish" speaking. It was mainly due to our household life changes that English became the main household language. I will explain more as I go on with my story.

Somewhere along the way I had a hard time speaking out loud and couldn't get the words out! I really don't know what happened to my speech but perhaps the adaption of the two languages I was forced to learn and speak by my father played a major role in my stuttering; in addition to the chaotic environment and household turbulence I was subjected to. It got so bad I lost all my speech motor control! Ugh I couldn't pronounce my words and had serious prolongation of sounds, I was lost vocally and felt like no one could help me. I always got teased and told to shut up! My mother never took me to get help for my speech disorder. She was told it will go away in time and that's exactly what was given to me nothing but time and a hard one at that. She would slap me every time I started to stutter, she would slap my mouth and tell me to slow down, breathe and restart. Needless to say; that didn't help. That just pissed me off and I started to really experience anger and rebel against everyone who laughed at me or thought there was something wrong with me. And to make matters worse, all my family members made fun of me too.

My trust in people started to fade quickly as the pain of embarrassment set in. So, what did I do? I stopped talking altogether. That's right! I thought I will teach them! I won't talk for some time. Maybe they will see how much it hurt me and then help me not to stutter. Well that didn't work I just became more introverted. I felt all alone now and knew that I had to do something to be heard. In time over a few years and determination to prove I could do it and to hell with everyone, I learned on my own how to calm myself down and get the words out. Today I am happy to say during my rise into employment and a long professional career, I have been able to be heard as a leader and strong speaker whether in a large group or small setting that, no one would even think that at one time I had such a terrible stutter problem. It's a good thing too, because I needed my fast savvy tongue to get my way through life on many occasions and who could do that by stuttering lol, yes, I can joke at myself about it now. But back then you can imagine how this made me an easy target for the other kids to make fun of me not being able to clearly say my words. I dealt with the bullying, teasing and harassment. This experience led me to fighting, as I had built up anger and resentment throughout my adolescent years.

As a young girl growing up even through all the turbulence at home, I got good grades, excelled in all my studies and was placed in academic classes from elementary through high school. Studying was always easy for me. I love knowledge and enjoyed reading books to no end. Absorbing information keeps my analytical mind content. I had a very short fuse towards bullies, shit-talkers and naysayers which in turn got me in trouble and yes kicked out of school a few times.

I grew up with a man in the house we called father. After his tragic death being shot by police officers, we came to know he wasn't mine or my sisters' biological father. He was only the biological father of one of my little brothers. My world came crashing down. I was confused. This was my first encounter with death, and it left me mortified. Who would take a child to an open casket funeral and then demand that he be touched by me? He was cold and hard and as I looked closer, I could see that there was something not right with the way his eyes were closed. This freaked me out especially because I was just told he was not my father. Who was my father? Where was he? Is he dead too?

Not too much was said about him until the age of 14. Then one day, out of nowhere, he came, my biological father came into town. He gave "us" meaning myself and two sisters the opportunity to meet him for the first time. I felt like what for and why now, so I declined and to this very day, I have not seen or met the man and I still feel no urge to meet him. He left when I was one years old and now, he comes back when I'm fourteen? What are you kidding? Being 14 growing up in Gary is like 25. I don't know you. Where were you when we needed protection? Or money or clothes? I really didn't have any feelings towards him because he was a stranger, I had no recollection of him in my life, so it was easy to say no. I wasn't angry I was just empty. I had no emotional connection to reach out to him. From time to time I would say to myself aren't you a bit curious? Am I a complete cold-hearted person? Nope, I'm good. I can't fake nor will I try to please others. It is what it is. You don't deserve my presence at all! I feel like my father died a long time ago and that's rightfully so since the man I remember as my father and took care of me until the age of 9 until he passed. A father is not always biological. So, any De La Rosa's reading this book and live in Texas we may be related. Here I am. Not afraid to meet extended long-lost relatives. I love a good story hence this book.

To make matters worse, my birth given name was Bertha. Yes, my name was "Bertha". Right? who names their sweet baby girl this name I thought. Ugh, I cringed every time my name was called. I would watch everyone's faces as they would say Berrrtha? Oh ok? … Geeze, I thought, just say it already, I know you think it's funny! I got teased a hell of a lot having that name. I don't know why it bothered me so much as it was related to being; a "big boned" and "overweight" person to people who didn't know its origin. I was like a skinny little bird. Which became my nick name since I disliked being called Bertha so much that the nick name Bird seemed easier to hear. So, I introduced myself as Bird to everyone I encountered and throughout my school years. I even wrote it down for teachers to call me this for roll call.

Bertha is an old Ancient Germanic name meaning "bright famous". Hhmm maybe there was something stirring in the cosmos when I was given my birth name. However, I felt it was too old of a name for me in the era I was living. I knew I couldn't go through life with this name. I had dreams and wanted a name people would remember. I asked my mother where this name came from as I got older and she said it was my grandmothers name from my biological father's side so I should be honored. Still feeling a detachment to this name, when I became of legal age and had a little money, I changed my name to Destiny. Sorry Mother I had to do it. The name Destiny was not heard of or popular at that time for some one's first name as it is today. After all I always felt I was destined for greatness. I received intrigue reactions from people when I say my name is Destiny. From the day I changed it, I felt alive and ready to tackle the world. It fit me and my journey to moving forward in life…" My Destiny".

Still with me? Ok my last stretch in Indiana.

I now come into the ah-ha moment when I start to understand what beauty means and how boys view me as a girl. My Mother moved us out of Gary and into a more highly populated suburban neighborhood. What that really means is we left the gang territorial neighborhood. I was now in Junior High School. I was in amazement of my surroundings! I found the blonde hair blue/green eyed people I had seen on TV in abundance. I stuck out now in this race of mainly all Caucasian looking kids. I felt funny in my stomach when I would look at the boys here. That's it! I was confused, interested, and aware for the first time I felt an instant attraction to them. I realized I would get angry and blush all at the same time when they would look at me. Ah well, then I thought, maybe it was because I wore a leather jacket, carried a switch blade, hair wild as can be, full on makeup, and I was a bit stand-offish at first introduction. Oh yes, I had my ways of the street about me so adjusting to the 360 environment I was thrown into was not an easy transition. I watched everyone's movements like a hawk, I was very quiet most of the time, cursed on a regular basis especially if I didn't like something. I took cigarettes and liquor to school as if that was normal. Fighting was like second nature. I had space issues and did not like anyone in my space unless invited. Much like my life today…but we will get to that.

I was told many times throughout my childhood what a pretty little girl or how cute I was but never gave it much thought until I started to experience boy harassment, flirting coming onto me and constant battle fighting off boys not knowing I was pretty or what the hell they wanted. I was a bit of a tomboy yet loved to dress up like the older girls around me. Remember the story about the bike chase, well I then understood what they were wanting to do to me and my sister if we were caught, yup and it was not going to be asked but taken.

Growing up in the tough streets, boys and girls grow up a bit faster in the show me yours and I will show you mine arena. The older boys were always trying to touch, kiss and be your boyfriend and you're like no…you're stupid, stop go away! Or that's what you think until you learn about sex. Ah-ha! So that's what makes the world go around and I got one!! Yes, the big "V" word came into play at a young age. I thought hmmm, do I use this to my advantage or hang onto it for dear life?

Fast forward into the mid 80's. I wanted to attend a college after I graduated. I knew my grades were good and I was smart enough to get in. I wanted to know more about things outside this small town I felt confined too. I felt I had become narrowed minded and stuck. My life was over. This is it. A small-town girl living in Indiana. A racist town with nothing to do but gossip and tell the same stories over and over. I asked my mom to please help me apply to a college after I had graduated. My mother didn't know how or have the means of providing me with any tuition financial options. My continuation to attend a collegiate school fell to the wayside. I started to work at an early age with odds and ends type of jobs. I felt defeated, so I partied a lot to kill the pain inside. The party life was everywhere. The mid 80's was exciting, I mean it was the era of rock hair bands, weed, kegs, cocaine, and psychedelic euphoria drugs. I managed to barely make it through this time period without becoming dependent on some type of substance drug. The racial slurs, propaganda, sex, drugs & Rock and Roll was at their all-time high. By age 17 I was working steady after school at a gyro sandwich shop and was able to buy my first car. A Dodge Charger for a whopping $500 bucks. I think it was a 68' and it was a badass. And by age 18, I had my first boyfriend and my first real relationship when I met the father of my children during my last year in high school before I graduated. I became discouraged not being able to attend a college and not knowing how to pursue it on my own. I knew I always wanted children and decided why not now. If I can't continue my education, then I will start a family.

The drugs were bad and the life of the '80s was not slowing down. I was becoming a pretty mess. I decided to become a young parent at the age of 19 and planned my pregnancy. I had my first son, then 13 months later my second son. The relationship with the father grew extremely toxic. I wanted out. I left him. If you have been listening so far you would know that no one was going to control me, beat me or degrade me unless you wanted to be six feet under or in the hospital.

My oldest sister was the initial driving force. She gave me the push, the will, and the strength to move out of this state. She left, I left. I left the state of Indiana around the age of 22 with a new boyfriend whom later became my husband. I thought my life was going to get easier, I was wrong. Dead wrong. So wrong and I have the next 30 years to talk about how I ended up back here.

So, where are we at now? My character was built here in the streets of suburban Indiana. I'm was 22 thinking I could tackle the world. I got my babies, my new man and a second chance on life. Yes, I'm free to move about new territory, explore and taste new foods, meet new people, live free of violence and choose my surroundings. Little did I know I was just about to experience more of life's painful adventures.

I do believe from our past we are built, driven and molded by it. Whether we are running from it or improving on it. It is the core of your existence. It will hold you down or move you forward.

Over the next 30 years my values remained as a straight shooter, protector, mother, girlfriend, and besties to some. I became divorced, fought endless and lost legal custody battles with the father of my children, moved to 3 states before I settled in California for 22 years and became a production guru businesswoman, traveled 10 years in parts of Asia, graduated from Fashion Institute Of Design & Merchandise FIDM school, purchased my first home on my own, and was considered a "Fashion Diva".

Then…BOOM! It all comes to a halt. My health went on a downward slope. Nothing life threatening but enough to slow my role from the harsh countless hours in the workday and a hectic role as Director of Operations in the Apparel Fashion Industry. So now what? This is what I'm good at. In my profession I was sought after, I got the job done. Now my hands are tied, I needed to get my health in order. I mean after all it's just a job, right? But it took one phone call to my son in Indiana to discuss my health and how it was abruptly ending my career and lifestyle, and just like that the decision was made. My youngest took this as his opportunity to have me in his life once again and more permanent. He was determined to have me move back to his home State where he resides, Indiana. He talked to me about how he was building and purchasing a new home and I was more than welcomed to live with him. He had the space and resources to help me get back on my feet. But all along I knew what he really wanted was "mom". His mother in his everyday life again. I knew he missed me. So, there you have it; I sold my home in California and you guessed it, I moved right back to Indiana to be closer and reunited with my two adult sons who now lived in Indiana and Chicago. Indiana was the medium ground between both regions. This allowed me to be near my precious new grandbabies, and to reconnect with my son's whom I dearly loved and missed. This is what I now call my second life "Glam-Ma".

My life took a full circle to the that place I vowed I would never step foot on again. I never looked back but fate or shall I say destiny had other ideas for me. Was this destiny's will with my name on it? What does it want? What's it telling me? I guess we will find out soon enough. My second life as Glam-Ma has just begun and I'm ready to tackle what it brings.

Come On! Follow me and my gypsy soul, restless of confinement making my life non-routine and more colorful then even I was expecting. Together let's see where it leads me next.

The best way to find the end is to go back to where you started…Indiana 2020.

Chapter 3

LIFE ON A COUCH

~Tricia Lynn

So, I got the call. Finally, I got **"that"** call. The long awaited, yet anticipated call. It's been almost two years, and my phone didn't ring. But today it did.

As I danced around my office and my eyes filled up with glorious tears, could it be, could this mean that I am now a free woman? Before I knew it, my feet started thumping and my body started moving, I was dancing with tears of joy around the office. I was finally free of the loveless, sexless, narcissistic controlling marriage I had been plagued with for over 20 years. I am Officially Divorced!! Can I get an AMEN!! No more degrading insults, like being told how useless, worthless and insignificant I am, no more being disrespected on a regular basis, no more being a married single parent, and most importantly, no more sleeping on the dam couch! Seriously, what is the point of being married if you must do everything yourself. Whatever happened to your spouse being your partner and not your ruler? My now, ex-husband just never got that memo.

Now, when I say I danced around the office; what I really meant was, I cranked up the volume on my cell phone as I held it up by my ear, and let me tell you, I danced up and down the halls, in and out of everyone's office singing at the top of my lungs, Kool and the Gangs

"Cel-A-Brate Good Times Come On". I held that phone up like it was an "Old Skool" Boom Box! Is that wrong? Lol...I think not!

It was at that very moment, when I was singing, that I realized I should have listened to my Auntie. My Auntie always told me: "Don't marry someone if you don't like their mother because your life will be miserable, you Must get along with the mother". After the first day I met "The Mother" I knew she and I were not going to get along. I don't like drama and her middle name was Drama. Literally if you looked up the word drama, I am sure her picture is there. Save the drama for the Llama and No Thank You!

I mean, when you stand in the middle of your 29 year old sons apartment, filled with his friends, corporate co-workers and my entire family shouting to him: "I'm your #1 lady, I gave birth to you" all because she was in the bathroom and didn't get to sing and cut the cake, you know there's going to be some issues moving forward. Seriously Lady, you are his mom, not his woman.

I mean really, unstable much? And the sad thing is there is nothing you can do but put your big girl panties on, take a deep breath, smile and yell out: "Who wants a SHOT"? It was time to defuse the situation after being utterly embarrassed and do damage control before my guests become more utterly disturbed. And did I fail to mention that I was sick as a dog and had a 103 fever while all this drama with the soon to be mother in law was going on. Shortly after the drama settled, his mom was so offended by not being able to sing and cut the cake, (or smoke in my apt.) she left and took her husband and crazy friend with her. Thank the good Lord...Peace has now been restored to the land. Ah fun times!

So, if you're wondering how I met this crazy family that turned my life upside down, well it goes a little something like this...

It's June 1996, and that is where the fun (cough-hacking) began. I took a two-week temporary assignment as an Administrative Assistant at a cellular software company in Chicago. Now, generally, I don't date people I work with. You know the saying, "Don't shit where you eat". Those were words I lived by. But then one morning I noticed Mr. McDreamy (well that's what I thought he was at that time) and he had me at a low. He was kind of a looker so, I thought to myself, well I am only going to be here for two weeks, it's been a while, so why the hell not. At lunch one day, I slipped my business card into his burrito bag. Was I having a momentary lapse in judgment, (obviously) or simply just in lust with this guy and wanted him? But let me tell you, I don't know if you have ever seen the movie Pretty Woman starring Julia Roberts and Richard Gere, but that scene where she returns to the upscale boutique that once snubbed her, after spending thousands at every other boutique BUT that one), Big Mistake...HUGE! Yep that is what I feel like now...HUGE Mistake in slipping my business card in that stupid burrito bag, HUGE! Clearly, I most definitely had taken a shit where I ate.

My two-week assignment turned into a six-week assignment which turned into the President of the Company creating a position for me and then offering me a full-time permanent job. Of course, I accepted, and this became the beginning of the next 23 fun filled years of my life and mostly sleeping on a couch in my own damn home.

I hadn't been on a date in almost four years (don't worry, that's a whole other story), but what you should know about that is that the guy I was dating before my now ex-husband (oh how wonderful that sounds) had really done a number on my head meaning, he mentally fucked me up and I had decided that I wasn't wasting one more second of tears, sweat or heartache on another man unless he was marriage material. Not to mention, by the time I got back on my feet and ready to hit the dating world, of course the guy I really had been head over heels in love with and wanted to marry since I was a teenager was sadly not available.

I had met him, the love of my life when I was about 15 years old and I instantly fell in love with him and became very close with his mother. We dated for a little while, but it didn't last long. Mostly because he was a city boy and I was from the suburbs, but more importantly, my dad was a cop and he just didn't approve of the relationship. This made it difficult for us to be together, so I just stayed away from him to keep the peace. And then sadly, one day his mom called me to tell me, the love of my life was getting married and that there was going to be a wedding, and I was not the bride. At this point I felt, all hope is gone, so why not go on with my life and date Burrito Boy.

Dating Burrito Boy came at a price I was not ready for. It was like a tornado with no warning, but you kind of keep standing there hoping it will pass you by without harming you. When I look back at the abuse I tolerated from his parents with the majority of the abuse coming from his mother, I sometimes wonder how I survived the abusive demeaning behavior and insults from them, I smiled and ate my food every time his mother burned it on purpose, I looked the other way when Burrito Boy drank himself into a stupor, which was often, and I often ignored the advances from his older brother. More importantly, I tolerated his obsessive controlling behavior, and the need to be with me always thinking wow, this guy really likes me, not realizing this was an unhealthy relationship. I didn't know that being in a healthy relationship means your partner would trust you enough to let you still have a life with your dearly loved friends and family without suffering any consequences. However, this type of toxic thinking that I had put upon myself had me alone and lonely with no friends. If it's one thing I learned and that is to never ever give up your friends because when your man leaves, your friends aren't always there anymore.

Being a young vibrant and single woman, I so wanted to have a great relationship. Isn't that what every girl wants? It seems that everything I did was just not good enough for him or his family. Sometimes it seemed as though these people (his family), seriously had seven heads and my facial expressions, I am sure, added fuel to the fire. Now, I will admit and take full responsibility for my facial expressions, they are just uncontrollable. I guess you can say, I wear my feelings on my face, and I suppose the faces I made whenever these people would behave the way they did probably didn't help my situation at all. I'm quite sure my facial expressions often gave the appearance that I was looking at them as if they had 7 heads. Well, and rightfully so, because they did. I mean if you act crazy, I am going to give you the side eye as if you are crazy. My face is a show and tell type of face, period.

I distinctly remember one Christmas Eve, when his mother had requested a restaurant style cheese grater for Christmas. We drove all over to find that thing and ended up having to travel an hour away to get it from a specialty store for restaurant kitchen gadgets. Well, she got exactly what she asked for but when she opens the gift and sees what it is, instead of saying "thank you I really wanted one of these", she turns to her husband and tells him to stick his penis in there so she can make dick cheese. Really lady?? In front of the entire family on Christmas Eve, you request dick cheese from your husband. Seriously, who does that? Can you imagine what my facial expression was for that one? It was a total look of disgust and confusion. And that's just one story of the insanity of this family that thinks things like this is normal. I could go on about the toxicity of the mother, but that was only half the problem in our relationship. So, moving on and back to Burrito Boy, shall we?

Ah…the commencement of the relationship and the first date with Burrito Boy. Dare I tell you what the hell got me into this fun-filled whirlwind of a fucked-up relationship. Well it all started with Italian food. Yep good ole, great tasting pasta. After all, remember, the love of my Life was getting married to someone else so why the hell not go on a date. This guy had balls of steal and thought our very first date should be a weekend away, at a hotel. According to him it was just to talk and to get to know each other. Yeah…Ok buddy, sure. Now I know I was born in the morning, but it wasn't THIS morning pal. I am 100 percent positive talking and getting to know me was not exactly on his agenda. Against my better judgment, I thought, why the hell not. I'm single, I'm free, I can handle this, and besides; hotel, free dinner, free breakfast, ok I am in. What? Don't judge me, he planned dinner at this great Italian restaurant, and I love Italian. Plus, I'm still thinking; hotel, free dinner, free breakfast, ok I am still in. But I have to be honest with you, about five seconds after I said yes, I will go, I regretted that choice because I got to thinking, who plans a hotel night for a first date, and tells you about it, but again against my better judgement, I went on this so called "date" of illicit intentions, even after I stressed over this all week and almost cancelled. I kept saying to myself, screw it, just do it, it's only dinner and I'm hungry right, it's only Italian right, it's only to talk and to get to know each other right? What could go wrong. Decisions, decisions, what's a girl to do?

Apparently, nothing. Thankfully my Va-JJ did the thinking for me "Amen and Amen again", my female organs said BAMM, you have company. FLO came to the rescue. She visited my vagina unannounced during dinner and said: No Hanky Panky for you tonight!! That's my girl. No woman likes to come on her period in the company of a man but talk about FLO having perfect timing was the perfect alibi for not having sex on the first date. Thank the good lord I now had a stress free no questions asked OUT!

Although FLO bum rushed my body organs that night, we still stayed at the hotel that night. However, he did not go to sleep happy, but it was a huge relief for me, and can we say, "free breakfast", that's all I really wanted at this point. But I must admit, he did take it like a gentleman, so I decided to go out with him again. Plus, let's not forget….it was a two-week assignment and I didn't think I'd be staying at the job much longer, so I figured no harm no foul. By the way, did I mention that the dinner was delicious?

Things were ok in the beginning of the relationship and we were having fun and then it quickly became a little weird and overwhelming. I saw the signs, but I don't really think I was paying much attention, like every time we went out, he would go out of his way to try and make me jealous just to see my reaction. When that didn't work (because I really didn't like him all that much) he immediately became very controlling. It was if, he wanted me to say something or to become enraged with jealousy as to validate his behavior. I literally saw him all day at work, had lunch together and then he expected me to drive 45 minutes every night to hang out with him at his house after work and then drive 45 minutes back to my house late at night. This started to get old for me real quick and I wanted to say to him: Ok, Buddy, how about giving me a break a couple nights a week or better yet, how about throwing me a couple of bucks for gas money if you are not going to take me out?" I thought what a cheap ass! Yeah, Yeah, Yeah,

I know you are probably saying by now, didn't you see this as a red flag, or are you catching the warning signs girl? Yes, I saw the flags and warnings, but like most women, we keep hoping it's going to get better over time.

We worked in Corporate America with several coworkers being our same age, so we did do a lot with that group of people which was a lot of fun. Outside of that he seemed to only want to go out with his friends and never mine. His friends, might I mention, were of a completely different breed. I did not have anything in common with most of them and the girls were rude for the most part and very immature. We just had nothing in common. His friend's idea of fun on a Friday was sitting in someone's garage drinking crap piss water for beer and acting like idiots, kind of like in High School. My friends and I were much more social, cultural and outgoing. We liked to go out dancing, attend art shows and galleries, dining, going to see musicals, etc. Our idea of having fun was not getting wasted in someone's garage. Just as an example; one year we were invited to a costume party at his friend's apartment. The only requirement to attend this party was to bring your own booze and an appetizer to share. I was excited for us to go to this party and meet some of his friends, so I made us custom costumes. I thought I had all bases covered; costumes – check, freshly prepared appetizer, check, cooler and cocktails packed - check. All is in tow and ready to go.

We arrived and then I saw it as soon as we walked in, yep you guessed it, we were the only two people in costumes. Yep, just us! In addition, who was the only one to bring drinks and appetizers? Yep, just ME! At this point, I just had one question: "Where is the freaking Halloween Party at"? It was obvious that this was not a party. This night consists of a few idiots playing video games and a few other idiots watching porn in the other room. We left after about 30 minutes. Um, thank you, but NO THANK YOU!! Just so you understand what I mean when I say my friends are so not about that garage beer drinking life, our idea of having a good time amongst each other is going to downtown Chicago for a nice dinner and then going to a musical afterwards like when we went to see the musical Joseph and the Amazing Technicolor Dream Coat with Donny Osmond. Are we seeing the difference yet in the caliber of friends? I surely was. Now make no mistake, I'm no high maintenance snob. I'm happy just going for a cup of coffee, maybe some breakfast or grabbing a burger. But McDonalds and Old Style in the garage is just not my thing.

Why did I keep dating him you ask? I'm not sure. Maybe because the love of my life found someone else and I was starting to think, I mean I wasn't getting any younger and I wanted a family. So, was I just settling, or could it simply just be the sex, although I have had better? The sex may not have been that great but at least back then it was often, and the foreplay was kind of fun. Who the hell knows why I stayed; I just did. I mean, he was a very selfish lover. It was always all about him. No passion, no love, no kissing... just sex. Don't get me wrong, I'm sure we all love a good pounding occasionally, but some love and passion occasionally is much better, for me anyway. I guess since the man I wanted to call my husband and have children with was no longer available and I figured all hope was lost, I thought to myself again, I wasn't getting any younger (pushing 30). At the time, he seemed to be marriage material for me, or so I thought. He had an education, a decent job, he served in the Marines, wanted kids, he was very good looking and had tattoos. I thought, Perfect! All the things I was looking for in a husband. I sure Thought Wrong, didn't' I?

The world revolved around his mother and his friends. He was always worried about what everyone else thought and making everyone else happy. I didn't think the same way. After all the things I had been thru in my life to get to where I was, I could give two shits what anyone thought. I was me. Take it or leave it.

Well, we ended up getting engaged after all the madness. Getting to that point was crazy (par for the course), but we did get there. The events leading up to that point were a bit reeling, but the actual proposal, believe it or not, was nice. Between the office girl ruining the surprise and telling me that he had bought me a ring and was going to propose, his sister in law trying on my ring before he gave it to me and his mother announcing she thought he was going to commit suicide because I was forcing him to marry me??? (really? we've been together 3 years now, but OK?), I can't even believe we got engaged. Apparently, I was color blind and all those red flags appeared white!

I started planning the wedding. Since we were paying for it all ourselves. I did not consult with any of the parents for anything and only put our names on the invitations. We decided that we wanted to do it our way and invite who we wanted. Well, THAT didn't go over well. My response was...too damn bad!! You don't want to help? You want to just cause problems? You get no credit!! My parents helped with what they could. His parents only wanted to help if they called the shots...they wanted stipulations; thanks, but no thanks. We don't really need to go into all the wedding etiquette violations that took place, I mean that could be an entire other book. I could go on and on about how his mother invited her own guests without asking, spent a small fortune on bringing relatives here from another country and paid for their travel and accommodations yet refused to be a part of helping with a bridal shower even though it was a combined shower with guests from both sides of the family. Then didn't want to help with the rehearsal dinner because she couldn't choose the venue and only wanted to invite her own guests. But I won't. However, she was utterly embarrassed when her relatives found out she wasn't helping or participating with the shower and they made her feel like shit. Then ALL OF A SUDDEN, she wanted to help and contribute. I held my ground. I did not cave. I told her and her husband to keep their money and their control issues, I didn't need them. Nor did I want them. They were still all included, and all were invited, however I did not take one single penny from them. Anyone that didn't like how we did things, didn't have to come. It was just that simple.

The wedding day itself turned out to be a lovely event and went off without a hitch for the most part. Mostly because I refused to let the In-laws from Hell ruin it. I refused to deal with them that day. Any issues they had, had to be referred to my father, not me. This worked out perfectly since nobody wanted to deal with my dad's temper and he had had quite enough at this point and wasn't letting any of them ruin my day. The evening ended up going quite smoothly.

We did however have an unexpected visitor at the wedding. A few weeks before the wedding I became very ill and collapsed at work. I ended up going to the hospital thinking I was dying of some rare flu virus, to find out...after I just went for my first fitting for my wedding dress, that we were in fact pregnant. Of course, I started to show the week before the wedding so not only did my dress need to be taken out, they had to put a panel in on each side. YAY ME!

It was nothing shy of a miracle that my first daughter even survived coming into this world. There was nothing but complications from the very beginning. As soon as I found out I was pregnant, complications officially commenced. My body didn't produce enough progesterone to hold her in. I was not producing a lining. I needed to take hormone suppositories that I had to keep in the freezer. They were specially made. We won't go into detail as to how and where they were deposited into my system, I'm sure you can figure it out, and let me just say…YUCK!! They made me so sick. I constantly threw up and didn't sleep. I had to take those for the first 3 months. Then after her first ultrasound it was discovered that she had developed something called Fetal Renal Pelvic Disorder and she was going to be born with complications to her kidneys, bladder and ureter. The ureter was not attaching properly, and everything was backing up.

I then was put on High Risk and had to start going to Loyola University in Maywood Park, Illinois, about a 2-hour drive from where I lived, for Level 3 Ultrasounds. They needed to be able to watch the flow of all her fluids. Everything seemed to be progressing however they were certain she would need surgery shortly after she was born.

Then came the food poisoning. Somehow, I suddenly became deathly ill. I was starting to shit blood. I went to the Emergency room and shortly after I was admitted they were able to test a sample of whatever was coming out of me. It was discovered that I somehow, ate shit!! LOVELY, right?

We had been looking at houses because I did not want to bring my new baby home to a third-floor apartment in Chicago. We stopped at a friend's and ordered some ribs. So, someone didn't wash their hands before handling my food. DISGUSTING, all I visualize in my head is some nasty ass person who was preparing my food, wiped his ass with his bare hands and then smeared it on my ribs. Just hearing it made me vomit in the hospital room. They put me on some major "safe for the baby" antibiotics. But Still, DISGUSTING!!!

Shortly after that, Now I'm still only 6 months pregnant, I started cramping, bleeding and feeling abdominal and back pain. Back to the hospital I went. Yep, now it was premature labor. The fun never ends! I was given some medication to stop the labor and laid in the hospital bed for a week. This happened twice. FINALLY, the doctor said I didn't have to go back to work since I had so many stairs at work and it was an additional premature labor risk. Woo Hoo, yeah me. I was never so miserable in my life.

There was a total of 2 good months of pregnancy, no pain, no hospital visits, no sickness, and FOOD! Food was suddenly, Wonderful!! You made it; I ate it. Green beans and mashed potatoes, milk and lots of it. Meat, Meat and more Meat. Then, the belly exploded, and the fun of eating crashed. Now, back to uncomfortableness, heartburn and no sleep.

She was supposed to be born on Halloween. She came into this world the first week of October. I always knew they were wrong on the due date and THANK the good lord for that or I would have given birth to a baby whale. She was 7 pounds and 12 ounces and 22 inches long. Can you imagine 4 more weeks of growing?

That was a baby delivery experience from hell, that's for sure. 15 long grueling hours of labor, 3 hours of trying to push, 2 epidurals (neither worked), her heart stopped at one point and they had to stick electrodes in me and into her skull to zap her heart back into rhythm, the cord was wrapped around her neck not once but twice. I had to get on my hands and knees, rock back and forth and roll around until at least one level of cord unwrapped, then the doctor had to reach in there and unwrap the next layer. I could feel and hear myself tearing. I mean skin, tearing, OUCH!! At one point before all the critical events took place, I commented to her father that I think she's coming out and he starts screaming PUSH!!! All I could think of was Shut the hell up and go get a doctor! FINALLY, she came out. They immediately put her on top of my chest, and I had never felt so much relief and overwhelming love all at the same time.

Unfortunately, that only lasted for a few seconds and then they took her from me immediately. Her color wasn't right, at first, she didn't cry, but then the whaling soon began it was like music to my ears. I remember at that moment not wanting anything to do with my husband anymore. My Va-Jay Jay was screaming, don't let him near us/me again. My only concern was that little life I somehow just managed to bring into the world.

She was whisked away to the neonatal unit and they immediately started working on her. Then they immediately started working on me and putting my Va-Jay Jay back together. I needed so many stitches that I believe I now had a bionic Coochie. They had the technology, and they rebuilt it.

The doctors told us that our daughter could not be at a day care and needed round the clock monitoring until her condition was more stable so I had no choice but to give my notice at work and quit my job that I loved and give up my opportunity to get my degree through work. My disability was about to run out as well, so I ended up giving my notice.

Ladies, here's some info you might find insightful in the event you have never given birth before. After they clean your baby up...they then climb on top of you and start pushing on your stomach. My doctor was literally on my bed, on her knees kneading my stomach like she was making dough for a pizza crust the size of my living room. All I want to know is, why does nobody tell you this crap. Speaking of which, ladies, if you've never given birth, you will shit on your nurses and doctor during a natural delivery. That's right, I said it. I'm putting it out there. Somebody needs to fill new moms in. I am happy to be that person. Ladies, whatever is in you, will be coming out of you, every time you push. So, there you have it. Consider yourselves officially fore warned.

It was all worth it to me. I felt the best job God could give me was to be a mom. This was my opportunity to be a better mom then mine was and maybe show her what I felt a mother's unconditional love should really be like.

My life since having children consisted of, well, them! My oldest has always been a high maintenance child. She was sick as a baby. She didn't sleep for several years, so of course, neither did I. Let her cry it out they said. It will only last a couple days they said. Oh Bullshit...you people clean up the explosive SHIT, literally, that was all over the crib every time I tried that torturous trick. This child would scream until she crapped herself, and it would be everywhere. There was no way I was leaving her in that shit…no pun intended. So, until she was about 5, I slept with her. Every single night. Was this the right thing to do? Probably not. Listen, nobody is happy if the Momma and the baby are NOT sleeping and if Momma's not sleeping, she's not happy. If Momma's not happy... ain't nobody gonna be happy!

Her father worked all day and then went to school at night. He was a stranger to her. She never really bonded with him as a baby and he never tried when he was home. He couldn't handle it. I'd leave her with him to go to the grocery store and five minutes after I got there he would call. The only sound was that of her screaming and then he'd say, come home, I can't handle this. Only to have to go BACK to the store later because Hellllooo, we still need food! I know, the simple fix would have just been for him to go shopping or we all go but you know…that would be too easy.

This child rarely slept at night. Then would take two, two-hour power naps during the day. Momma started napping with the baby. When she slept, I slept. Life revolved around her sleeping schedule, which kind of sucked and most people made fun of me for it but whatever! Lack of sleep will make you insane. It is a proven fact. After a couple years of not sleeping, I believe I may have snapped two or three times.

It turned out she had developed something called "Night Terrors" when she was about 8 months old. She would awaken about an hour after being asleep, screaming bloody murder, and her eyes were closed. She was still asleep. This sometimes would go on for forty-five minutes at a time throughout the night, and for several years until she eventually outgrew it. She was born with a bad case of Billy Rubin and her ureter was not connected properly. The first two weeks of her life she endured an extensive number of tests that were often invasive and traumatizing. She was stuck with needles every day for a few weeks. I had to bring her to the hospital every day for almost a month for blood tests and we lived an hour away. She was connected to an ultraviolet belt for a couple weeks. I called her my little glow worm. Things eventually corrected themselves and she never needed surgery thankfully but that sure as hell was difficult.

That experience was definitely an eye opener for me, and I knew then I had made a huge mistake on the man I chose to marry and start a family with, aka Burrito Boy.

It was the second episode that my daughter had of her night terror attacks. Her bedroom was only a few feet from ours. I could make it down the hall in less than 3 steps when I was in full on "Super Mom the Savior" Mode. I heard her start screaming right away. I still had no idea what was wrong, I picked her up, couldn't get her to stop screaming and as I started to walk down the hall to bring her to our room, he had gotten up and closed the bedroom door on me. CLOSED THE DOOR ON ME!!! Are you Fucking kidding me right now? I of course kicked the door open while holding the baby, YES, I was in full on exhausted psycho new mom mode, and then proceeded to kick the bed calling him all kinds of colorful loser names. It was that moment, I'll never forget, 20 years ago, I knew I was doing this shit by myself. From then on, I became a married single parent.

Shortly after my daughters first birthday, I had to move. I was miserable. My husband was gone from 6am to 11pm Monday thru Friday. I was alone, in the middle of nowhere, no friends or family, no help and a baby that didn't sleep and cried ALL THE TIME. I put our townhouse up for sale and sold it in 3 days. I was outta there!!

We moved into a nice 4-bedroom tri-level home in a great neighborhood in the Northwest Suburbs of Illinois. Things finally started to get a little better but only because as my health got better, it wasn't as difficult to take care of a baby growing into a toddler all by myself. My father had relocated back to Illinois from Florida to help me and I was finally able to breath a bit and take a flipping nap. Then he got sick.

He was diagnosed with Esophageal Cancer and it eventually took him. I struggled severely, he was my best friend and the only man I could ever count on and the only one that was there for me no matter what. His funeral turned into something right out of a Jerry Springer Episode, we won't go into all that right now, but it was ugly. I went into a deep depression after that and became highly medicated. They did not help my situation or make my husband less of an asshole. They only made me numb so I didn't feel anything or react uncontrollably to the madness. They don't make the problem go away. I needed to take care of my daughter, and myself. After a few months of walking around like a zombie, I decided to self-wean off the meds and anti-depressants.

Thank the good Lord I made that decision when I did. The next thing you know...BAMM I'm pregnant again. I was grateful to not have that crap in my system so as not to contaminate my new baby.

Health wise as far as this baby was concerned was all good. But for me, not so much. You see, I was like super craft mom, a "let's have all the kids in the neighborhood over" kind of mom, did I mention I could scale a tree in 3 seconds flat? Did I also mention I can fall out of one even faster? A few months before I got pregnant, for the second time I had the neighborhood kids over doing crafts and making Chinese lanterns out of tissue paper, watered down Elmer's glue, milk cartons and Christmas lights. Being the gymnast that I am (cough cough, what...? I did gymnastics when I was a kid, doesn't that count?), I scaled up the tree in my backyard to hang the Chinese lanterns. Unfortunately, I didn't come down as easily as I went up. I slipped, fell out of the tree, landed lopsided on a log with one foot on the log and one foot off, Smacked my head on a landscape ornament gifted to me by my Monster in Law (I truly believe she was secretly planning my demise with lawn ornaments in addition to food poisoning).

Come to find out 3 months into my pregnancy that I had shifted my pelvis months earlier in that fall. The weight of the baby growing in fact tore the ligament holding my pelvis together in front and the ligament dissolved leaving bone on bone making it impossible to walk. I was basically bed ridden and in excruciating pain 24/7. My husband continued to work full time and I continued to NOT have any help from either side of the family. We had just moved to the area, so I also had no friends yet. Thankfully another mom from my older daughter's preschool was an absolute God send and helped get her into and out of school and to and from my car for me. I am forever grateful to her. I could not have gotten my daughter to school without her help.

I struggled through the next seven months but somehow survived and gave birth to a beautiful little girl. I had to have an emergency C-section as once again, she started coming out early, but If I had her vaginally, I would be paralyzed forever. The contractions began and I drove myself to the hospital.

Caring for her while trying to heal proved very difficult. It was difficult to hold her for a while. It was too painful to hold her and walk. I needed therapy to be able to walk again. We had a lot of stairs which also proved near impossible, all the while trying to care for my then five-year-old, and a newborn. Did I mention my five-year-old decided, a week after my C-section, to run over to the neighbors, jump on the trampoline and snap her tibia in half so she was in a full-on cast from toe to thigh. The release nurse at the ER said to me: "Now she'll need to be carried to and from the bathroom, it's a no-weight cast". I thought (out loud) "Are you KIDDING ME…I have absolutely No Help", I just had a C-section and my pelvis is separated. I had to call someone to come over just to get her into the damn car to even get her here to the ER! Yeah, that's not happening.

Needless to say, we set up camp downstairs by the closest bathroom and I quickly learned the crawl and scooch techniques to get her to and from the bathroom and me up and down the stairs. Then I just broke down and borrowed my grandmother's walker on wheels with a flip seat so my 5-year-old can wheel herself around the house. Like all things, the girls and I managed to get thru it. I just kept telling myself. This Too Shall Pass! Fun times people, Fun Fun Times!

And it did pass, until years later when my oldest daughter came home from therapy one day and told me her therapist referred to me as the "Sacrificial Lamb" of the family. It took me a long time to understand what that meant. Without trying to home in on my girl's session and have her divulge her therapy secrets. I thought hmm, well what the hell does that mean?

Yes, she was in therapy. She was just shy of 17 years old at the time. She was sad, exhausted, not sleeping and just generally in a bad mood. We had finally resolved all her sinus issues and infections and years of antibiotics. She had to have maxillofacial corrective surgery on her sinus's after an injury in 8th grade where she was kneed in the face during a softball game. She often was sick a lot. At one point she had been on and off antibiotics for over a year. She was finally recovering and then this.

I decided at one of her regular doctor appts. to discuss some of the changes I was observing. The doctor asked her how she was feeling, and my daughter responded that she didn't want to live anymore. She had watched her father and I fight and argue for years from his lack of help, support and involvement and she felt very unloved and uncomfortable around him. Legally of course, the doctor has no choice but to act on that and of course my heart fell out. She was put on antidepressants and I was made to search out counseling for her. If we didn't get her to a counselor, they would have admitted her for a psychological evaluation.

Her father was unsupportive. He said the doctors were crazy and she didn't need help and he wasn't paying for therapy. Thankfully the first few sessions were covered by insurance. After that, getting him to pay the bill was absolute torture. That fact that he refused to support her getting the help that she so desperately needed set her back even more. The antidepressants continued up until and thru the first few months of her freshman year in college.

My daughter went to a private catholic college prep high school. The pressure and the expectations of the students was very demanding. She also was 100 percent into the theater program there. It was exhausting. Her father never supported anything we did.

My kids both went to the same catholic grade school. He always complained about that. The man made six figures, yet we were always broke, and he never wanted to do anything to help make sure our kids had more opportunities to become successful well rounded educated functional adults.

Since the kids went to a catholic school, volunteering was mandatory. Over the course of the fifteen years as a school family, he never stepped foot in the school. Mostly, because you know, he worked, that was his "sacrifice" as he called it. I think from the time my oldest was in kindergarten until the time my youngest graduated, I volunteered all my time and he never set foot in the school unless it was an emergency. I was on most committees at one point or another. I chaired the art auction for many years, I worked on the art projects with the students, I was a volunteer art teacher for the "Meet the Master's" program, I helped run the Halloween fun fair, I worked recess duty (once and that one was not for me), I was in charge of creating the school yearbook, I was a volleyball coach for eight years and organized the "Play for Pink" events, to name a few. I also volunteered at church as a Eucharistic Minister for many years, I was on the CRHP team for five years, and served on the arts and environment committee decorating the church for a while. I also was on the dinner dance fund raising committee and helped raise thousands of dollars for both the church and the school.

I know it sounds like I'm bragging but I'm not. Trust me. Just trying to point out the difference between my involvements vs. his. Which was ZERO.

He never took them to the doctor, the dentist, to school or any extracurricular activities. It was all me. I'm not even sure he knew where the front door was. He never knew the kid's teacher's names or any other information for that matter.

When the kids at one point tried to sit down with him to tell him how they feel and why they don't feel loved by him, a lot of what is mentioned above was brought up and his only response to them was that they don't appreciate the sacrifices he makes for them. Really? What sacrifices? The fact that you have a job. That's a sacrifice? Are you kidding me? He'd have to have a job with or without us if he wants to eat. All I can do is shake my head. He will never get it. We call him Princess. That is his nickname. The world revolves around him. His main concern is making sure he has everything he needs; his hair and clothes are perfect; the fridge is filled with the foods he likes, and we do everything he wants, or we don't do it at all. At one point he said to me in the middle of an argument that "the world does not revolve around the children". My response was "Well MY world does!" Hence the nickname "Princess". I mean, God forbid he drop us off at the front door of a restaurant in the rain. If his hair is getting wet, then so is ours. Who cares that it's Easter and the girls are dressed in their Easter dresses and bonnets, carrying gifts?

Oops, I got off the sacrificial lamb topic. Sorry, I do that sometimes. Just try and keep up. Sometimes I skip around.

I looked it up and the definition of Sacrificial Lamb is a metaphorical reference to a person or animal sacrificed for the common good. The term is derived from the traditions of Abrahamic religion where a lamb is a highly valued possession.

Well I'm sure as hell glad part of that definition means I'm a highly valued possession but not so sure exactly to WHO? My kids, but certainly not my ex-husband. Not even so sure my immediate family either. Certainly, wouldn't be able to tell by their actions, that's for sure.

I'm thinking what she meant was I did everything. I gave up my life, my friends, my job, my chance to continue my education and get my degree, my independence and well, everything. I gave it all up to be a wife and a mom. As the kids got older, it just got worse. It really was mostly the three of us against the world, and him.

And now that I have divorced Burrito Boy and my girls are growing into womanhood, I can't help but to think…what do I do now. Do I love again, do I dare step out into the dating scene, do I dare to begin a new life for us.

Stay tuned for the next Chapter in my life….

Chapter 4

ME, HIM, THEM AND THEN I

~Rebecca R.

As I put on this parachute, and as I made the decision to jump out this damn plane at my age, I could only think, where would I be today if I had not taken charge of my own life? Where would I be if I had stayed in a lifeless marriage as a hostage to my own menace of a decision. But NOT today! It's my birthday weekend and I am rejoicing in the paths of my ways and the rebirth of my joyous life as me. How wonderful is that, could it be I'm free from the chains of a once loving marriage that turned into a mental bondage? But NOT today...I'm flying high and I am jumping!

I am a strong woman, who was raised by a man alongside two very strong brothers. So, my personality is assertive. I never learned how to beat around the bush with anything, although I can be gentle; I just do it and I just say it, thanks to the strong men in my family. But as all women do, we do have soft spots, cuddle corners, and we love hard. And sometimes we unintentionally screw up and love too damn hard.

I don't know when I fell in love with him, but I did. I was a sophomore in high school, and he was junior. We had a class together, and he was smitten by me, as he should have been. I was a hot buttered biscuit and fine as hell. He asked if he could sit by me in our assembly hall, I said: "Sure". He asked if he could put his arm around me, I said:

"Sure". So hmm, seems like he trying to butter this biscuit…lol. I knew I didn't have nothing to worry about because if he tried anything funny, I had my daddy, my big brother and my baby brother to beat him up LOL!

Thank God no bones were broken, because I married the man of my dreams at the time. I was madly in love with this man, in fact I loved him so much that I enabled him to the point I just couldn't love him anymore. Sounds confusing right? I know what you are thinking, how can you love a man so much that it ruins your relationship or to really make it twisted, how can you love a man so much that you realize, you just don't love him anymore? Behold, it happens, and it happened to me.

Although I live a wonderful life now and I give all the praise to God for giving me the strength and the courage to ask for help and to act on that help, because I believed in the higher power so much, that I knew I could step out on faith. I stay prayed up!

After forty-one years, two children (ages 25 and 36), five miscarriages, three dogs, and four cats later; he turned out not to be the one, the man of my dreams. How in the H E double hockey stick (HELL) did I get here? And yet the funny thing is, I know it wasn't a waste of my time. I truly loved him; I mean I LOVED him. Do I need to say that again? Oh, what the hell, I loved him!

Hell yes, there were times that I knew I should have left him. But I am a praying woman, and I know God said: "Here she comes again". That's right Lord, I'm back. But as a woman and a mother you contemplate so many times how to get out of a bad marriage, you go from saying to yourself: "What about the Kids? How will I Survive? Where will I go? What will I do without him"? And it all makes sense, until you lose yourself in the madness and the pain and sadness has you so deep in a depression that you don't know yourself and you sure don't recognize yourself. So, if you don't know you, then who does? This eventually leaves you open like an open wound for salt to be constantly poured on you until you are too numb to heal.

But after so many tears, numerous infidelities and several yeast infections and an attempt to take my own life. I woke up and said: He is not worth it! Now can I say that again…Hallelujah! **HEEEE AIN'T WORTH IT!**

I honestly can't tell you when he stopped loving me, because there was no big red flashing sign saying; WARNING! I, me, myself and I had to wake my own damn self-up. I think I prayed so hard and so much, that I just had to put my faith to work. God was not going to do it alone. You can ask for help, but "you" must take the first step, you must walk alongside him, and not be lazy about it. If you call on him, you better be prepared and ready when he lifts you.

Whew, that was a rough time in my life, although he gave me the most beautiful kids that are the love of my life, I still have to say thank you for giving me them. There was a time when I divorced their dad, and it was a little rough because they didn't understand why after all this time, or why now, or who do we choose to be with, or what happens now. I am sure they were mad at me, and I am sure their father was devastated when I made the choice, in fact he was because no one saw it coming. But now time has healed the hearts and if my kids love me and understand the freedom that their mom needed to be a woman again, and just to have life again, as they say…I'm good.

But what about being single and free, what do I do now, I still want sex, I still want to be loved, and I am still a hot buttered biscuit at my age…lol. I look good, I feel young and free. Because remember I met him as a teenager, and he was the only man I had ever had sex with. I knew the love of no other man. Dating, I had not dated in over thirty years. Boy am I in for a treat, I guess.

At this point my brain or my "Kitty" (vagina walls) started speaking to me. What you "going to" do Rebecca, you are free, single and ready to mingle? I just knew I had to keep my head up and my heart open for me and Kitty to meet Mr. Right…lol.

So, let the dating season begin. I was ready for sex, ready for love, ready for a relationship or whatever. I wanted something different, something fresh, I wanted to be treated different, I wanted to feel free and more importantly, I wanted to explore life, a new womanhood.

As I started to step out on the dating scene, I tried my hand at dating apps, and yes, I met some crazy people, and a few nice people, and made some friends along the way. This was starting to be fun, and honestly, I was having a good time in my new single life. But of course, you always meet that one guy that thinks God parted the red sea, and he just came gushing out.

This one guy I met was so in love with himself and his penis that he was King to himself. Let's just call him for now Mr. Tap Out, and you will soon see why. I met him on a dating app, and we started chatting. He would always talk to me about what he was going to do to me sexually, and he would say he was going to make me "tap out". Well in the boxing world, he should be so good sexually, that I would "tap out" as to say "stop" I can't take anymore, or I would just give up. Then he proceeds to ask me if I want to see what he's working with. So, in the real world that means; penis picture coming my way…lol. I simply replied: "No, I would rather see it in person".

Thinking yeah, ok, if we ever get to that point. Then I started thinking, I have only known you for 72 hours and you're already talking like this, then it's a no brainer because we both know what you want. So, I decided to remind him that his profile mentioned that he was looking to build a relationship with someone, but your conversation isn't even on point, it's totally different. My thoughts are, can you fuck my mind first with your words? But then I thought what the hell, let's meet to even see if we are even attracted to one another. Well that thought blew right out the freaking window because shortly after, braise yourself, yep...I got it. THE dreadful DICK PICTURE! The picture that every dude thinks we want, and we clearly don't.

What the hell! My Kitty is saying: "Oh no, is this what he working with"? So, this is Ms. Kitty talking, not me: "Is it even hard"? He replies: "Yes". Well I'll be damn. Ms. Kitty says: "No thank you. You just made me mad. Thought you was going to make me "tap out"? Not with that! Now see, if he had just let us meet first, maybe the attraction for each other would have made it a little better, and Ms. Kitty may have been more preceptive to the smaller things in life. If you know what I mean. The only thing I could say was: #boybye.

The good news is that I continued to date, and I was starting to become a pro at the dating scene. It made me realize I still had it. I felt good, I looked good, I was confident and free; what a great place to be in my life. And what's even better is that I started to enjoy sex again, so much so that some men, did not get a call back from me the next day if they were not good. I mean really, I am fresh out the pen and you give me that. Ms. Kitty wasn't happy, and if she not happy, well you got to go. But there were some guys who taught me some new tricks, and for that I thank them. I truly believe sex is needed and should be enjoyed – especially if it's done right.

However, the sex that comes with benefits, in other words as we say; friends with benefits. That shit doesn't work because someone always catches feelings. And I sure did a couple of times, and that don't feel too good. That's when Ms. Kitty steps in and say look, we need to talk. Ah! The joys of the single life.

Now, as I sit on my personally designed Zen patio in Arizona, miles away from that other life that held me captive for so long, I'm reminded of how thankful I am, to just live again. I am so grateful to be loved, and to love life again, and to love my kids and be loved by many as I love them. I can't remember when or if I ever felt this before.

My new life is the beginning of a future. Now I can live my life the way God has intended it to be. And that is truly happy, knowing that I am ENOUGH!! Because there was a time, I never thought I would get through the mental abuse, because it may not be physical, but it can leave everlasting scars if you let it.

Although I am still a work in progress, my spirit is much brighter. Even though at times I may get lonely, which I now know is perfectly normal, I quickly correct myself because I am never alone, I walk with God. God is forever present, watching and giving me the strength that's needed to go on.

My love for God is deep, and it's His love that sustains me. I was once told recently by a man that I thought I could build a life with that I was too assertive, meaning "having or showing a confident and forceful personality". It's funny, many years ago I would have curled up and been submissive, and settled, but today my response is: "YESSSSS, Bitchhhhh - I Am"!! I love who I Am!! And I can't nor will I ever water myself down again to make someone else feel comfortable.

Every day I am learning to be at peace with myself and to sit still and wait on God to bring me that someone special. So, as I fix me, he's working on me, and the thought of knowing I will find that one, keeps me sane. But in the meantime, I am going to continue dating, skydiving, taking trips, drinking great wine, enjoying life with my friends, and continuing to make beautiful memories with my two amazing children as we embark upon this glorious life together.

Until my next Chapter…peace and blessings!

Chapter 5

THE HAIR SLAYER

~Kimberley G.

Today I am known as Ms. Kimberley from the hard knock streets of S.E. Washington D.C a.k.a the infamous short hair slayer in the Nation's Capital. But let me tell you, it was not easy getting here, and my life was not "easy peasy". At the beautiful single, sexy and sultry age of forty something I would say I am happy, but I would love to have someone to share my success with.

Growing up as a little girl in my grandmother's home without my beautiful mother had its challenges and as I recall I was always a little fast at growing up and always curious about my life. With a grandmother being very settled and still, I pretty much had to venture out on my curiosity. I remember being curious about life and my sexuality at a very young age, just from watching older adults around me. I precisely remember being about five- or six-years old thinking that I had a nice body.

You may wonder, what does a five or six-year old know about having a nice body? I just knew I was sexy and chocolate with beautiful brown skin, and everyone said I was pretty. So, when the time came for me to act on my thoughts of sexuality and having a beautiful body, I did it…I flashed my little naked body at a little boy I knew, and he just turned and walked away. But victory to me, I did it, and I was not afraid; and then it hit me, what was I doing. I later had to whip my own ass in my head about me being fast and grown. You know how the elders would say to your mother, she is just growing up to fast; and that is the thought that had crossed my mind. But those thoughts didn't last long. By the time I was 11 years old, I thought I was a fully-grown woman. Nobody could tell me I wasn't, besides I had already flashed someone, so I felt, I made it into womanhood.

Not yet quite twelve years old, I managed to snatch my first boyfriend and I wanted to kiss him, but he didn't want to. He was afraid of a kiss, but he had a cousin that was not afraid of anything. His cousin told me: "I will kiss you". It was at that moment I realized now here's a man, so I thought…lol. He's not afraid to act like a grown up so, I broke up with my boyfriend and started going out with his cousin. It was just that easy and we used to kiss all the time, with tongue and everything. But he wasn't as nice as his cousin, my first boyfriend, so I quit him just like that and found myself going back to my first boyfriend whom I had left because he wouldn't kiss me. But after a while I was ready for the next big thing and I asked him for sex. My boyfriend said: "If I didn't want to kiss you, you know I am not going to have sex with you". And once again his cousin stepped up to the plate like a little kid raising his hand saying: "I'll have sex with you". Now that I look back at it, I think that was the beginning of me choosing or being selective over who I give my body to. Surprisingly, what you learn as an adult from the things that you endured or went through when you were a child. Certain moments in your life can be so crystal clear and you can remember the precise moments of actions and movements.

I was 12 years old when I had sex for the very first time. I remember the encounter distinctively because I was in the seventh grade and the boy I had sex with told me that he would get sick and his dick would fall off if I didn't do it to him. Well I couldn't have his dick fall off, I had to save him. Now that I look back it, I should have let it fall completely off because the very next day he told everyone. Can you imagine being in Junior High and the entire school knows you just had sex? It was so bad that even the teachers knew. My PE teacher called me into her office and counseled me about the incident and then told me I had to tell my mother, or she would. What a snitch! But I was so embarrassed. When I went home, I'll admit it, I was so scared to tell my mom, but I had to, and I did. I never really knew if she was mad, angry or just glad I told her, because she immediately put me on birth control. Ironically, due to that traumatic experience, I couldn't get myself to have sex again. The whole time I was on birth control, I never had sex. I think it was safe to say, I had learned my lesson. But that lesson didn't last long, because as soon as I got off birth control, I was fucking ninety going north. Years passed and I acquired a few different partners. All meaning not much to me at all. But the experience of having sex and wanting something different started to change.

I was now an adult and just turning 24 years old with a new boyfriend. I honestly don't know how it happened or why, but my boyfriend at the time brought one of his friends over and sex exploration went to a whole other level. I had a threesome and it went down so fast, I didn't even see it coming, nor did I stop it. It wasn't planned, but it was a wild night to remember. It was new and adventurous, and I felt safe because after all he was my boyfriend and I figured he knew what he was doing. I trusted him. Not sure if that was good or bad but I did.

Trust and Love! You know what they say: "What's Love Got to Do with It". As I got older, I started to realize I had a lot of love to give, but it was never reciprocated. I often found myself going above and beyond to satisfy the needs of the men I was with, but my needs were either ignored or they simply just didn't care, or could it be these men honestly did not know how to love a woman, and more importantly, how to love a woman the right way.

Men treating a woman correctly or loving women the right way seems like a myth or a dream that you hope to find one day before you die. I was once madly in love with a man, that actually turned out to be one of my longest relationships, but he never chose me to be his wife, "the chosen one", because he was a Muslim and I would not convert, which was his requirement to marry me. I had been wanting and waiting for him to choose me for a very long time, and to this very day we are only friends but in today's time we call it FWB (friends with benefits) which basically means, friends with sex on the down low with no intention on being in a relationship. I was so in love with this man, and wanted so much to be with him that I gave him money, redecorated his home, and anything else he wanted me to do, but none of that was good enough to be chosen to be his wife and to make matters worse, I was not that satisfied in bed. But as we do what we do as women, sometimes we settle for less because that vagina talks, and it makes us feel all mushy inside and we give in because we care. But as for now we are still FWB and the sex can be amazing now because I have trained my body to have an orgasm before he releases. It took a lot of work to train him on how important my happiness was. I needed better love and better sex; it was just that simple. I mean a girl's gotta do what a girl's gotta do.

I think it's fair to say by now that sex and I are a match made in heaven. I just simply love to fuck! Yeah, I said it! In its most vulgar sense. I've always enjoyed having sex. I have had two great encounters with sex escapades; once when I was in high school when me and my boyfriend would go around the corner to my aunt's house and fuck during lunch break, and once when I was in my 30's my boyfriend and I had sex almost every day for six years. And surprisingly to this day, I still can't find no one to match my sex drive. Many have said my sex drive is so high because I have a "white liver" (whatever that means) or I'm just freaky because my zodiac sign is a Scorpio. But whatever the reason might be, I still want to have sex, and mostly with the same person continuously and plenty of it. However, in some strange way, I have never desired to sleep around with plenty of men.

That's the great thing about being single, you have the freedom to date who you want and have sex with who you want and when you want. But when it comes to having a sexual drive as a woman, you become the "W", a whore as some call it. But it's different when a man has a high sex drive, he becomes "The MAN", it's always a double standard when it comes to women and sex.

Mostly, what I have learned from the power of the "P" is that it can be a blessing to the right man and a curse to another. But what I do know that as a single woman living a single life today, I believe that if you don't control the emotions, the needs and the wants, in other words, give it some attention, you will find yourself settling for what comes your way rather than waiting for the right man that is supposed to be in your life.

But I still want sex, and lots of it, so I will continue to be a little picky until I meet Mr. Right. My journey in life does not end here, in fact, it's just beginning.

ABOUT THE AUTHOR

I have lived, loved, and cried all from this irrational and emotional beast we call the "Vagina". It has bought me Joy and Pain in my 55 years of life. But the good news is, there is not much I would change except for a few ex's here and there. But from pain comes growth and possibilities. I am no longer a victim of mental, physical and sexual abuse. I am no longer a victim of the life I was dealt. I am now a "Survivor" and I know how to say: Thank You. Thank you to those sons of bitches that exited my life and thank you to those beautiful souls that entered my life and gave me a brighter hope and a brighter future. I am a mother, a sister, a friend, a grandmother, a lover, an undiscovered comedian, a writer, a kickass businesswoman, but more than that...

I am Life!

www.ingramcontent.com/pod-product-compliance
Lightning Source LLC
Chambersburg PA
CBHW061337040426
42444CB00011B/2970